MW01260025

THE LION KING

TWENTY YEARS ON BROADWAY AND AROUND THE WORLD

By Michael Lassell

A WELCOME ENTERPRISES BOOK

EDITIONS

LOS ANGELES • NEW YORK

HALF TITLE: *Jorge Lau as Mufasa, Mexico City, Mexico.*

TITLE SPREAD: *The triumphant ending of "Circle of Life" from the Mexican production of* The Lion King.

Copyright © 2017 Disney Enterprises, Inc.

Oscar and Academy Award © Academy of Motion Picture Arts and Sciences
Grammy © National Academy of Recording Arts and Sciences
Tony © American Theatre Wing and The Broadway League
Tarzan® owned by Edgar Rice Burroughs, Inc. Used by permission.

Page 78: From TLK Opening Night PLAYBILL. Copyright © 1997 Playbill, Inc. Reprinted by permission of Playbill, Inc.

Page 89: From *The New York Times*, December 7 © 1997 *The New York Times*. All rights reserved. Used by permission and protected by the Copyright Laws of the United States. The printing, copying, redistribution, or retransmission of this Content without express written permission is prohibited.

All rights reserved. Published by Disney Editions, an imprint of Disney Book Group. No part of this book may be reproduced or transmitted in any form or by any means, electronic or mechanical, including photocopying, recording, or by any information storage and retrieval system, without written permission from the publisher.

For information address Disney Editions
1101 Flower Street, Glendale, California 91201

Produced by Welcome Enterprises, Inc.
6 West 18th Street, New York, New York 10011
www.welcomeenterprisesinc.com
Project Director: H. Clark Wakabayashi
Art Director: Gregory Wakabayashi
A GREG / CLARK DESIGN

ISBN 978-1-4847-7376-5
FAC-04115-17288
Printed in Canada
First Hardcover Edition, November 2017
10 9 8 7 6 5 4 3 2 1

FSC MIX Paper from responsible sources FSC® C016245

PHOTOGRAPHY CREDITS

Anita and Steve Shevett: 164

Brinkhoff/Mögenburg: 8, 39 (right), 128, 132, 134–135, 168 (left), 185–187, 202–205, 223 (left)

Deen Van Meer: 6, 34–35, 38 (right), 94–98, 100–107, 110, 112–119, 125, 126, 129, 130, 136–139, 168 (right), 180–183, 190–193, 223 (right), 224

Disney Theatrical Productions: 163, 165, 170, 184, 215

Frank Veronsky: 140

Gilda Villareal: 1, 2–3, 90–91, 210–213

Guzman LLC: 162

James Morgan: 108–109, 121, 151, 188, 189, 201

Joan Marcus: 23, 83, 88, 124, 158, 222 (right)

João Caldas: 93, 120, 122–123, 127, 133, 207–209

Johan Persson: 178

John Hogg: 196–199

Katsuhiko Hori: 172

Kenneth Van Sickle: 11, 29, 31, 32, 36, 37, 38 (left, top and bottom), 39 (left), 41, 42, 44–71, 73–77, 84–87, 141, 143, 149

Kim Seung-Hwan: 194

Lois Greenfield: 222 (left)

Marco Grob: 27

Masanobu Yamanoue: 167, 174

Matt Crockett: 179

Matt Murphy: 40, 92, 152–157, 159

Mimosa Arts: 146

Per Breiehagen: 43, 131

Phillip Jarrell: 111, 214, 216–219

Stéphane Kerrad: 200

Steve Fenn/ABC/Copyright Disney 2010: 160, 161

Takashi Uehara: 176–177, 195

Tony Russell: 19

Whitney Cox: 72, 145

CONTENTS

HAPPY ANNIVERSARY

The Lion King at Twenty

Mufasa stalks the Grasslands, which are represented by members of the ensemble, in the U.K. tour.

An unqualified smash Broadway musical, as any producer will tell you, is downright miraculous. There are no exact formulas for success—though there are an infinite number of roads that lead to failure. So many elements have to fall perfectly into place; the odds are stacked against anyone intrepid enough to take on this challenge. A Broadway musical is the Mount Everest of commercial theater, and few who make the attempt ever reach the summit.

This is the story of the most successful Broadway musical of all time.

On November 13, 1997, Disney's *The Lion King*, which opened at the New Amsterdam Theatre on Forty-Second Street, achieved exactly the kind of acclaim that daydreams and backstage movies of the 1930s are made of. The popular and critical embrace of the show was so instant and enormous that it is hard to imagine now that its success was ever in doubt.

But this cherished and wildly inventive production faced adversity even before opening night: it slogged through all the unknowns of the musical theater development process, flirting with every pitfall and courting every potential disaster, just like every other show—successful and not.

On November 13, 2017, roughly a generation after its opening night: *The Lion King* reaches a rare milestone, becoming the third Broadway musical ever to celebrate a twenty-year continuous run—and it's still playing to full houses. (The other two? All right, we'll tell: *The Phantom of the Opera* and the 1996 revival of *Chicago*.) Oh, did we further note that Disney's Best Musical Tony-winner still consistently finishes at or near the top of the industry's weekly box office tally?

However, the story of *The Lion King* goes far beyond the financial figures it accrues and the ongoing impact the show has on New York City's entertainment scene. As of this writing, *The Lion King* has been seen by more than ninety million people on six continents. (If Antarctica had a theater and a significant population, it would probably be playing there as well.) The world has so far seen twenty-three productions in nineteen countries and nine languages—plus multiple national tours of *The Lion King*. It is one of only two shows in theater history to generate five productions worldwide that have had a run of ten or more years. And it has earned over $7 billion globally, which is more than any theatrical production or film title ever—for example, all the *Star Wars* movies put together.

And the audience continues to grow! In the past two decades, *The Lion King*'s North American tours alone have played in seventy-seven cities across the United States, Canada, and Mexico—and the number continues to grow!

Ultimately, the real measure of *The Lion King* is not its profit or its popularity. *The Lion King* tells its emotionally moving and uplifting tale in a production that reigns as one of the most purely theatrical events in the annals of modern stagecraft.

Given its critical acclaim, unprecedented revenue, and the affection audiences all over the world display, it is astonishing that *The Lion King* was only the second full-scale Broadway musical production that the Disney company had ever created. The first, *Beauty and the Beast*, which opened in 1994 (the same year *The Lion King* movie premiered), ran on Broadway for thirteen years, despite a less than warm welcome from the Broadway establishment and mixed reviews from the critics.

Equally surprising, perhaps, is that *The Lion King* was the very first stage offering produced by Peter Schneider and Thomas Schumacher, who today is president of Disney Theatrical Productions as well as its producer. Before they took Broadway by storm, however, these two theater-trained friends and colleagues worked as Disney animation executives and were intimately involved in the creation of *The Lion King* film from the moment of its conception in 1989.

This book is a celebration of *The Lion King* musical at twenty, a Broadway production based on a blockbuster animated film. It is also a look back at the long haul, from the creative team's first meetings to the show's opening night. And it's a bit of a family scrapbook, containing memories recounted by the people who have had the singular pleasure (and anxiety) of creating and presenting *The Lion King* in the United States, Europe, Asia, Australia, Africa, and South America. Many of these personal stories are being told here for the first time.

So, welcome to the party. Everyone's invited!

And here's to twenty more years of *The Lion King*. Long may it roar!

A WORD FROM THE PRODUCER

Mufasa (Cleveland Cathnott), Rafiki (Ntomblfuthi Mhlongo), and Sarabi (Balungile Gumede) in "Circle of Life," Hamburg, Germany.

I often ask myself why *The Lion King* works.

Of course, when talking about the stage version, my first answer is always Julie Taymor— the brilliant storyteller, designer, weaver of myths, and goddess of the theater. Without Julie there is no *Lion King* onstage.

But the story begins even earlier than that. For almost thirty years, every single day, *The Lion King*, beginning with the film and now the stage musical, has been a part of my life. Yet after all that time, and with this intimate relationship to the material, I continue to wonder this: Why does it work?

Why does the show work the same when I sit with an audience in Tokyo as it does when I sit with one in the Netherlands? Why does it work when I see a production in Johannesburg or Paris, or London or Hamburg, or Shanghai—or anyplace else that *The Lion King* has played? What is it about this show?

The Lion King certainly echoes the great fairy tales that have become major Disney films, such as *Snow White and the Seven Dwarfs*, *Cinderella*, and *Sleeping Beauty*. These are stories that scholars such as Bruno Bettelheim—in his *The Uses of Enchantment*—cite as cultural archetypes over the centuries.

It is also a legendary "hero's journey," a central theme of epic world literature that mythologists such as Joseph Campbell, in his *The Hero with a Thousand Faces*, analyze. Campbell's theory is that tales of heroes of all kinds, from Buddha and Krishna to Jesus, all share a common mythological root, a primal idea that affirms in man how experience transforms us from childlike beings into adults. Chris Vogler's guidance on the elements of Campbell were invaluable for us as we developed the film and in fact became the basis of his book *The Writer's Journey: Mythic Structure for Writers*.

In addition, *The Lion King* connects itself to innumerable primal mythoi, whether those are biblical narratives, such as the lives of Joseph and Moses, or great works of literature, from medieval epics to Shakespeare's plays. (That being said, five of us were in the July 2, 1991, meeting where Scar became Mufasa's brother, and I can assure you no one mentioned *Hamlet*. The tale of *Hamlet*'s influence on the story made for good press copy later on, however.) But of course these are fundamental elements of the human experience: betrayal, redemption, acknowledgment, and acceptance.

As *The Lion King* permeates through and distills the myths of the ages and the study of our common culture of storytelling, it fundamentally reveals that it is, surprisingly simply, a story of us—and therein rests its greatest meaning and deepest resonance.

What's fascinating is that no matter where you are, who you are, or what your circumstances are, it is an elegant and powerful allegory, a human story told with animals—but not of any specific location or real place, so each culture brings its own perspective to *The Lion King*. Everybody has family. Everybody has community. Everyone has to face this question of *their* responsibility for their family and community.

When do you own yourself? When do you take responsibility for who you are? And what do you do to set things right when you have made them wrong? It's a very simple tale, but it has enormous resonance in global history and experience, as well as in great works of religion and literature and in the ongoing human struggle with the meaning of our shared experience.

All of the academic analysis and scholarly interpretation of *The Lion King* is fascinating and legitimate. But for me, it is—and always will be—about the *people* who made it.

Walt Disney himself once asserted that you can design and create the most wonderful things in the world, but it takes people to make the dream a reality.

I was on a panel right after *The Lion King* opened on Broadway ("Working in the Theatre," which the late Isabelle Stevenson hosted for the American Theatre Wing). The panel was made up of me; Peter Schneider; Julie; Lebo M.; our publicist, Chris Boneau; and Rick Elice, who was then a marketing wizard for the Serino Coyne advertising agency and has since written *Jersey Boys* and other shows, including our own *Peter and the Starcatcher*.

Rick said something that started with, "Ten years from now, when this show is still running . . ." and all of us on the panel, along with the invited audience, laughed out loud. *The Lion King* in ten years? Impossible. And here we are, incredibly, not only still running, but still at the top, twenty years later.

If Peter Schneider and I, and Jeffrey Katzenberg, and Roy Disney, and Don Hahn and Roger Allers and Rob Minkoff, and a pile of brilliant animation artists had not set out on this journey, there would be no *Lion King* to contemplate.

When you go, as an audience, to see a film or a play, that's what you see. But when I see one of our films or shows, I see *people* I know. I know what they did.

Forever seeing the indelible mark of my friends, colleagues, and collaborators on every component of the finished piece is, for me, the truest joy of our work. Brenda Chapman, as head of story, shaped so much of the film. Chris Sanders, as a designer and storyteller, leaves a mark that can't be denied.

Peter and I know what Hans Bacher did by creating a series of small panel paintings early on that deeply influenced the opening of the animated feature (as well as designing, years later, the stage show's unforgettable logo). We know that Dan St. Pierre supervised astounding layouts that reinvented the way a "camera" works in animation. We know that Andreas Deja animated this, and Ellen Woodbury animated that. The idea that Rafiki is a baboon who carries that stick and has that expression, well that's a contribution from Joe Grant, long gone now.

In the stage show, I still look at "He Lives in You," Mark Mancina's brilliant song when the dancers all come on in their dashikis, and in my mind's eye I'm still watching Aubrey Lynch from the original production. I see Michele Steckler sitting next to us in the theater with her headset on, during our long tech rehearsals and then previews, to keep us apprised of each calamity onstage. I can sometimes *smell* the frankincense on Ashi Smythe, one of the original ensemble members, as he came down the aisle. I look at the bird women and I see the Dlamini sisters, two beautiful South African women who joined our ensemble in the beginning. I know what Tsidii Le Loka created as the original Rafiki. I see the remarkable Heather Headley as Nala and her Simba, the extraordinary Jason Raize, now sadly passed. I see Jeff Lee and Doc Zorthian and all the other people who made this miracle happen onstage; so many people who are also unsung, unknown . . . they're all part of this extraordinary event.

I see Don Holder behind the gorgeous lighting design. Richard Hudson created the most startling and stunning scenic treatment. Irene Mecchi, note pad in hand, running down the aisle with a change to make. Michael Curry was right next to Julie, delivering those astounding masks and puppets, and Michael Ward worked with Julie to create the extraordinarily detailed signature makeup designs for the show.

Can you even imagine the fortitude of the crew that made this show come to life? Nothing we did was normal on Broadway, but Drew Siccardi, Jimmy Maloney, Victor Amerling, Kjeld Andersen, and Louis Troisi honestly didn't flinch. They made the impossible possible.

Producer Thomas Schumacher consults with director Julie Taymor in the early stages of production.

The Lion King was given life twice: first by the animation team that created one of the most glorious films of all time, and second by an intrepid company of actors and technicians and designers and musicians who shaped Julie Taymor's stage version.

And that can never, ever, ever be forgotten. The people who have touched *The Lion King*, who created its rich and meticulous texture, this ornate and compelling tapestry, are deeply moving to me—because nobody in the audience really knows they're there.

Animation and theater are in many ways "arts of the invisible." The greatest contributions people make are so often unrecognized—they are, in fact, unseen. And every contribution any-one makes requires all the contributions that have gone before. The power of *The Lion King* is in that collective humanity.

Today *The Lion King* (with its iconic songs by Elton John and Tim Rice) appears around the world with a team that encompasses our various licensees and partners. It indeed takes a village. But for as long as most can remember, a gang of soldiers led by the indomitable Anne Quart—including Thomas Schlenk, John Stefaniuk, Anthony Lyn, Marey Griffith, Celise Hicks, Clement Ishmael, David Kreppel, Doc Zorthian, and a team of dedicated design associates (Mary Peterson, Peter Eastman, John Shivers, Louis Troisi, Jeanne Koenig, and Carolyn Wong)—has kept us together.

The irony is that *The Lion King* is a story with no *people* in it. But the whole power of what it has become lies in the vision, the talent, the commitment, and the passion of hundreds and hundreds of unforgettable people.

—Thomas Schumacher
President and Producer, Disney Theatrical Productions

PART I

THE BIRTH OF A KING

First There Was a Film

The Lion King, the number-one box office film of 1994 worldwide, was an overnight sensation. Disney's first Afrocentric animated feature, with its captivating visuals, emotionally uplifting tale, and congenial Elton John/Tim Rice score, became an instant classic, embraced by children and adults alike. Its principal characters have become so iconic that their images are among the most recognizable in the world. Before there was a global blockbuster, of course, there was a story, and before that, the germ of an idea. And that idea was formulated on an airplane somewhere over Europe in 1989.

"I have it in my mind that it was between London and France, but I might not be right about that," says Peter Schneider, who was running the animation division at the Disney Studios at the time. Schneider was traveling with

Jeffrey Katzenberg, then head of the studio, and publicist Kevin Hyson, doing a promotional tour in Europe for *Oliver & Company*.

"It was my first time in a private plane," remembers Schneider, "and it was very exciting. We were just talking about what was interesting about moviemaking. I think Jeffrey brought up Africa. And then started talking about his days as a teenager working for New York City mayor John Lindsay, and he brought up the idea of personal responsibility: 'What is our responsibility to our community? What is our responsibility to our fellow man? What's our responsibility to religion, responsibility to education?' And that was it—something about Africa and something about responsibility to a larger entity than ourselves."

Poster for the original release of Disney's 1994 animated film. Art by John Alvin.

"The idea for the story," says Katzenberg, "came out of an experience that happened to me that was about growing up. It was that moment in all of our lives when we go from being a child to being an adult."

The journey from that personal reflection told at thirty thousand feet to a finished film called *The Lion King* took five years. And the path through the jungle of possibilities was anything but a straight line.

There are not many people who have the distinction of midwifing both *The Lion King* feature and its Broadway successor. Schneider, though, is one of the few who can. Another is Thomas Schumacher, current president and producer of Disney Theatrical Productions. Before Schneider left Disney to create his own company in 2001, the duo ran the division together, but they had worked together long before that.

Schumacher and Schneider met in 1983, when they shared an office at the Mark Taper Forum at the Los Angeles Music Center. Schumacher had been at the Taper since 1980 and was co-running the company's Improvisational Theatre Project. Schneider arrived in 1983, to head the theater component of the Olympic Arts Festival, a massive citywide ten-week celebration of international arts scheduled around the 1984 Summer Olympics. Schumacher subsequently joined the Olympic Arts Festival as a line producer in charge of one of the festival's many venues, Schoenberg Hall at UCLA.

The Olympic Arts Festival, with its hundreds of performances and exhibitions at scores of Los Angeles locations, was so successful that a group of civic-minded arts organizers, led by Robert J. Fitzpatrick, decided to do it again in 1987 (sans the Olympics). Schumacher was hired as one of two associate directors of the event, which was being called the Los Angeles Festival. He was primarily responsible for programming.

Schneider by this point had departed for New York with his new wife, Hope Tschopik, who had been one of the directors of the Olympic Arts Festival. In New York, he signed on as the company manager for *Little Shop of Horrors*, the smash off-Broadway musical hit by Howard Ashman and Alan Menken. Schneider, however, soon returned to California, when he was offered a post as vice president of animation for Disney under its new executives, CEO Michael Eisner and Studio chairman Jeffrey Katzenberg. Both had moved to Disney from Paramount when Roy E. Disney, Walt Disney's nephew, recruited them as part of an effort to rescue the failing House of Mouse during a corporate takeover battle in the mid-1980s.

"I arrived in Burbank in 1985," Schneider remembers, "shortly after the release of *The Black Cauldron*, probably the worst animated film Disney ever made." Animation in general was at a low point, and many in and out of the industry wondered if the idea of doing feature-length cartoons had come and gone with Uncle Walt, who had died in 1966. Roy Disney, however, was passionate about the survival of animation, which he saw as his family's legacy. He was not going to let go without a fight.

Happily, things were about to change—and radically. "The release of *Who Framed Roger Rabbit* in 1988 provided the first clue," suggests Schneider. "The game changer, though, was the release of *The Little Mermaid* the following year."

THE LION KING TIMELINE—PART ONE

1989

November 17: Disney's "animation renaissance" begins with the release of *The Little Mermaid*

December: The idea of doing an animated feature set in Africa is articulated for the first time

1990

November: Animation chief Peter Schneider assigns nonmusical *King of the Jungle* treatment to animation producer Thomas Schumacher

December: Schumacher approaches Tim Rice about musicalizing *King of the Jungle*

1991

March 14: Howard Ashman, the force behind *The Little Mermaid*, *Beauty and the Beast*, and *Aladdin*, dies

April: Lyricist Tim Rice starts working with composer Alan Menken to finish *Aladdin*

June: Production on *The Lion King* film begins

November 22: *Beauty and the Beast* film opens

1992

November 11: *Aladdin* film opens

1993

February 8: Disney Theatrical Productions incorporated to produce *Beauty and the Beast* on Broadway

1994

March: Production on *The Lion King* film completed

April 18: *Beauty and the Beast* opens on Broadway at the Palace Theatre

April 26: *Beauty and the Beast* cast album released

May 31: *The Lion King* soundtrack album released

June 15: *The Lion King* film opens

September: Disney Theatrical Productions restructured with Peter Schneider and Thomas Schumacher at the helm

1995

February 28: Release of *Rhythm of the Pride Lands*, sequel to the soundtrack of *The Lion King* film

March 1: *The Lion King* soundtrack wins a Grammy: Best Musical Album for Children

May: Disney signs long-term lease for the New Amsterdam Theatre on Forty-Second Street

June 1: *Beauty and the Beast*, nominated for nine Tony Awards, wins one, for costumes

June: Schumacher proposes Julie Taymor to direct *The Lion King* musical on Broadway

October: Irene Mecchi and Roger Allers begin work on the book for *The Lion King* musical; Hans Zimmer and Lebo M. begin to work on the music

1996

January: Taymor travels to Orlando to present her production ideas to Disney CEO Michael Eisner

August 9: The first staged reading of *The Lion King*

1997

February 10: *The Lion King*'s "Puppet Workshop" at the Palace Theatre

April 2: Official opening of the renovated New Amsterdam Theatre

April 28: Tickets go on sale for the out-of-town tryout of *The Lion King* in Minneapolis

May 14: First rehearsal of *The Lion King* at 890 Broadway, New York City

May 18: A concert version of Alan Menken and Tim Rice's *King David* inaugurates the New Amsterdam; six performances only

June 15: Disney's *Hercules* film plays the New Amsterdam for two days

July 8: The first preview of *The Lion King* at the Orpheum Theatre in Minneapolis

July 31: *The Lion King* opens in Minneapolis; runs through August 31

September: *The Lion King* cast album recorded

October 15: *The Lion King*'s first preview at the New Amsterdam

November 13: *The Lion King* opens on Broadway and the cast album is released

After a perceived twenty-year decline in the popularity of full-length animation films, Disney had itself a huge hit. *The Little Mermaid* ranked thirteenth in domestic box office for 1989 and was nominated for three Academy Awards. It won two: Original Score (by Alan Menken) and Original Song (for "Under the Sea," by Menken and Howard Ashman). A second song, "Kiss the Girl," was the third nominee. Seemingly overnight, animation had reinvented itself—by marrying the Broadway musical.

Key to that transformation was Ashman. He was brought to the studio by Schneider and Katzenberg, whose friend and mentor David Geffen was one of the producers of *Little Shop of Horrors* in New York—more evidence that everything and everyone in show business is interconnected.

Schumacher had joined Schneider at Disney in 1987 as a feature animation producer; his first assignment was *The Rescuers Down Under*, a sequel to the charming and quite profitable *The Rescuers*. The sequel was not a box office success. But by that point Ashman and Menken were deep into production for what would turn out to be their opening trifecta of superhits: *The Little Mermaid*, *Beauty and the Beast*, and *Aladdin*.

The animation renaissance was in full swing, and in the midst of this creative whirlwind, Schumacher was given two new film projects to supervise: *Tim Burton's A Nightmare Before Christmas* and a low-priority title known at the time only as "the lion movie"—though it would soon be called (temporarily, it turned out) *King of the Beasts*. It was subsequently retitled *King of the Jungle*

A concept painting for the film explores the relationship between Simba and Mufasa. Art by Don Moore.

(until Roy Disney pointed out that the film did not actually take place in a jungle).

At the time Schumacher was named its producer, *King of the Beasts* was not a musical. It was, he describes, "a kind of animated *National Geographic* special about a war between lions and baboons, all set in this brown, dirty, earthy environment. Rafiki was a cheetah, and Scar was the leader of the baboons. And nobody had much interest in it.

"The A-list animators all chose to work on *Pocahontas*. It was actually my husband, Matthew, who first brought up the idea of adding music to the film."

"Rescuers Down Under came out after *The Little Mermaid,*" says Matthew White, the aforementioned spouse, who was once a ballet dancer and is now a highly renowned interior designer, preservationist, entrepreneur, and writer. "I felt so bad for Tom, and then he was given what sounded like a very grim new assignment while everyone else at the studio was all about the new musicals. And I said, 'Can't you at least make them sing, because that's what people like.'"

And Schumacher, who grew up loving stage musicals, thought, *Well, why not a musical?*

But the film's director and key studio executives were skeptical. Schumacher was steered to Tim Rice, the world-renowned lyricist who had recently come into the Disney fold when the studio bought the movie rights to *Evita*, which Rice had written with Andrew Lloyd Webber. As part of Rice's agreement with Disney, he would be "available" to analyze prospective film projects with an eye to musicalizing them. "So, in the fall of 1990, I sat down with Tim Rice in California and I laid out the story as it existed at that point," Schumacher recounts, "and asked him if our war between lions and baboons could be made into a musical. And Tim said, 'I made a musical about the obscure dead wife of an Argentinian dictator. *Anything* can be a musical.'"

To make a musical, of course, you need a composer as well as a lyricist. "Having popular music stars create songs for Disney movies is nothing new," Schumacher points out. "Peggy Lee sang on *Lady and the Tramp* and even wrote some of the songs. And Louis Prima's rendition of the Sherman brothers' 'I Wan'na Be Like You' from *The Jungle Book* is one of the most popular numbers in the Disney songbook." Because Tim Rice had had a good experience collaborating with them on the musical *Chess*, Schumacher offered the gig to Benny Andersson and Björn Ulvaeus of ABBA. There were months of back-and-forth conversations, but ultimately both declined to participate.

So, in the spring of 1991, Elton John was contacted as the "pie in the sky" choice. "Tom Schumacher said I could have anyone I wanted except Alan Menken," remembers Rice, "because Alan was tied up with *Aladdin*. To me, Elton was the obvious choice. It wasn't my principal objective to introduce rock music to Disney animation but to work with a great tunesmith, which Elton undeniably is. He writes wonderful melodies that work whether you treat them as rock songs or as standards.

"I do remember saying that they'd never get him because he'd be too busy and too expensive," Rice adds. Indeed, the nature of the deal Schumacher was able to offer John's managers, with its usual strict Disney ownership and copyright

A production still from The Lion King *film showing Simba under the paw of his Uncle Scar.*

provisions, did not fly; thus, in August of 1991, John and his management, too, passed.

After John's first response, he contacted Paul McCartney, who said no. Then Schumacher went back to Elton John, who passed on it a second time. With the story moving along from treatment to script stage and production set to commence—with, ironically, a director who didn't want the film to be a musical at all—the songwriting job was next offered to Barry Mann and Cynthia Weil, who had written the songs, with James Horner, for Steven Spielberg's *An American Tail*. The film's "Somewhere Out There" was the 1988 Grammy Song of the Year.

But Mann and Weil were a music and lyrics team, leaving Tim Rice out of the equation. That didn't please Katzenberg, who hopped on the phone and started pulling strings with the legal and contracts people about concessions to the standard deal memo. The result: Schumacher flew to London in October of 1991 to offer the film to Elton John a third time.

"It turned out that Elton and I lived about a hundred yards from each other in London," remembers Rice, "but neither one of us knew it." At the meeting, Schumacher and Rice laid out the story, and John accepted readily as if he had no idea he had already turned aside the proposition twice before.

"They really didn't have to sell it to me," remembers Sir Elton, who is himself a huge fan of *The Jungle Book*. "I mean, I was in from the word go. I loved the story and I loved that it was an original story, and it came at a time in my career where I wanted to do something different. Of course, the songs in Disney's animated films are legendary and classic, and so good that it was a challenge for me to rise to the occasion."

At the end of the meeting, John said he'd have the songs done by Thanksgiving.

> I think that whether you are writing for an Argentine dictator's wife or for a warthog with wind problems, it's the same approach lyrically. I just have to make sure that the words the character says are plausible (a) for the character and (b) for the story. And for *The Lion King* it was not as incredibly difficult as it can be because the story was very strong.
>
> 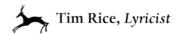 **Tim Rice,** *Lyricist*

In fact, it would end up taking three years of work on the lyrics and melodies—and nonstop revisions to both—before the score was completed! Why? Because work on *The Lion King*, the title that was eventually picked, was anything but smooth sailing, or a slam-dunk. Even before its completion, Schumacher was promoted to vice president of animation development and taken off day-to-day production of individual films. Don Hahn became *The Lion King*'s new producer.

"No one cared about it," recalls Peter Schneider. "It was about animals, which was considered impossible to sell. It didn't have a princess. It was very cheaply budgeted. It had no heat. There were tremendous production problems. Nothing was jelling. The story wasn't coming together. And no one liked the songs that Tim and Elton had written."

"When Elton sent us his second demo for 'Circle of Life,' after he'd been asked to rewrite it," remembers Schumacher, "Jeffrey Katzenberg listened to it and said,

'Well, what are we going to do with that? I mean, maybe it could be an end-credits song.'"

"Many people thought the songs were horrible," says Schneider, "and while I wasn't against the film being a musical, I was not convinced these songs worked. They were not theatrical. Elton's demos were all bouncy and one-note."

Rice, however, who was in the trenches with the production team shaping the story, as well as writing and rewriting lyrics, thought the executives were insane.

"Tim said, 'Let me sing them for you,'" recalls Schneider. "So we all gathered in a small conference room away from the main building with a couple of vocalists and Michael Reno playing the piano. And Tim Rice sang the songs. He sang 'Be Prepared.' His singers sang 'Can You Feel the Love Tonight?' And for the first time we realized, in Tim's passionate but very straightforwardly simple way, that the emotions carried the songs. He showed us that the songs were inherently theatrical."

Simba and Nala get tossed by giraffes in the film's "I Just Can't Wait to Be King" sequence.

The second major musical "aha moment" involved "Circle of Life."

"It didn't quite fit into the movie," remembers Rice, "or at least the directors felt that it wasn't working. And I was asked to change the lyric about two hundred eighty-eight times. All right, I exaggerate. I think I did twenty-three different lyrics—by no means every verse. But some of them were completely, radically different, and the song was given to various characters at different points in the process."

Given how internationally iconic the opening of *The Lion King* has become, it's hard to imagine how tortured its path was. Ultimately, the man who found the key to the film's completion was its composer, Hans Zimmer.

Zimmer had been hired at the suggestion of Roger Allers, who codirected the film with Rob Minkoff. Zimmer had written the score for a 1992 film called *The Power of One*, which was set in South Africa, and he had introduced South African music to that score to stunning effect. South African music had been emerging in the zeitgeist, in large part because of Paul Simon's hit 1986 album, *Graceland*, which featured the group Ladysmith Black Mambazo. Zimmer took "Circle of Life" as it was presented to him and called on South African composer Lebo M., who had worked on *The Power of One*, and singer Carmen Twillie to create what became the film version of "Circle of Life," marrying Elton John's pop song to the gently rhythmic South African chant called "Nants' Ingonyama," which was sung in the Xhosa and Zulu languages.

"That changed everything about *The Lion King*," says Schumacher. "It defined the movie." The movie had an opening number, a great opening number, that set the aesthetic and cultural world of the film in its opening note.

Katzenberg, too, was duly impressed. "Hans Zimmer," he has said, "is the single greatest artistic creative collaborator that I have come across in my career in the movie industry, and without him there would be no *Lion King*."

Even Sir Elton was thrilled, remembers Allers. "He got really excited about it. We had done a rough storyboard version of the scene put to Hans's score. By the end of the sequence, Elton was jumping up and down in his chair, he was so happy with it."

But "Circle of Life" wasn't the only song bothering the film's directors. *The Lion King* cut shown to Elton John in Atlanta near the end of the production process did not include "Can You Feel the Love Tonight?"

"So I said to Jeffrey," recalls John, "'This is a love song. Every animated Disney movie has had a great love song in it. You cannot leave this song out.' I was, I admit, very perturbed. I thought that leaving it out would be a mistake, and happily they listened to me and put it back in."

The Lion King was released on June 15, 1994, becoming one of Disney's greatest hits of all time. "Can You Feel the Love Tonight?" won an Academy Award.

This story sketch by Lorna Cook shows the reunion of Simba and Nala.

Disney Meets Broadway

Disney's media attention, meanwhile, was not only on movies and TV at this point. The company had ventured into the world of Broadway musicals with *Beauty and the Beast*—somewhat ironically, since this show was based on yet another movie that had not been conceived initially as a musical. *Beauty* opened at the Palace Theatre on Broadway on April 18, 1994.

It was Robert Jess Roth, a talented young director who produced stage shows for the Disney theme parks, who first suggested to Disney Chairman and CEO Michael Eisner that *Beauty and the Beast* belonged on a Broadway

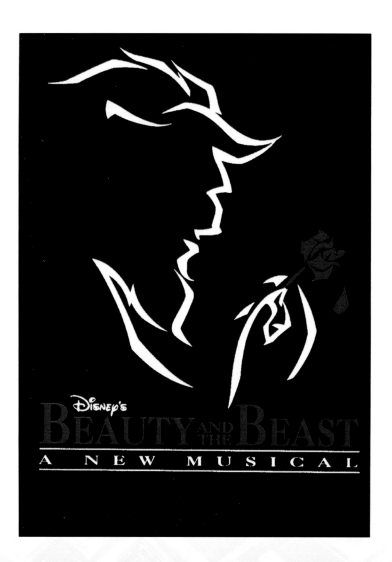

stage—a logical enough suggestion given that the film had been created by musical theater mavens Howard Ashman and Alan Menken. But Roth was not the only one who had thought about such a move. Frank Rich, head theater critic of *The New York Times*, offered up the opinion in a radio broadcast that the best Broadway musical of 1991 was not a Broadway musical at all, but Disney's animated movie *Beauty and the Beast*.

So, in 1993, Disney Theatrical Productions was incorporated to produce *Beauty* on Broadway. The president of the new company was Ron Logan, who had headed the live productions unit for the Disney theme parks. Disney Theatrical Productions' first Broadway effort opened the following year under the direction of Rob Roth.

Conceived to be as close an approximation of the film as was possible in an onstage production, the stage version of *Beauty* also featured additional songs and an expanded book with lush sets and costumes. Although its critical reception ranged from enthusiastic and grudgingly positive to condescendingly cool and even downright dismissive, *Beauty* was a box office bonanza.

The production wound up running for 5,461 performances before closing in 2007 and ranks as the tenth-longest running show in Broadway history. It was nominated for eight Tony Awards, including Best Musical, but won only a single award—for Broadway veteran Ann Hould-Ward's costumes, a result some attributed to the Broadway establishment's deep suspicions of Disney's motives for its foray into live theater.

The poster for Disney's first Broadway production, Beauty and the Beast, *1994.*

And that was supposed to be that.

But Michael Eisner had grown up in New York City and enjoyed Broadway musicals. He also liked making money for his company and extending its ambitions to new arenas of entertainment. So shortly after *The Lion King* film opened, he sat down with Peter Schneider and Tom Schumacher, who were by then president and executive vice president of animation, respectively, to discuss the future of Disney onstage, giving "the boys," as they were widely known, new responsibilities and the additional titles of president and executive vice president of Disney Theatrical Productions. And then he said he wanted to do *The Lion King* onstage.

"And I told him it was the worst idea I'd ever heard," says Schumacher, who then proceeded to ignore him. Instead, he and Schneider asked Elton John and Tim Rice to write the score for an original Broadway show based on the story of the Egyptian slave girl Aida, which had originally been proposed as an animated film.

Schneider and Schumacher set up a theatrical division, first in Burbank and later in New York, bringing on Stuart Oken to supervise and develop creative content for the new venture and Alan Levey as general manager. After that they started considering shows. "We actually started seriously developing *Pocahontas* for the stage," remembers Schumacher, "and *Mary Poppins*, which we did eventually produce. But none of us thought *The Lion King* would work onstage."

"We had always joked while working on the film," says Allers, "'Well, they'll never turn this into a Broadway musical. Can you imagine everyone hopping around in fuzzy costumes looking like animals?'"

Heather Headley, The Lion King's *first Nala, in the title role of* Aida, *Disney's third Broadway musical.*

Then Ward Morehouse, a columnist for the *New York Post*, wrote in his column that Disney's next stage venture would be *The Lion King*. "He had picked up on a joke someone told," says Schumacher, "and thought it was real. But people believed it and his column set up a kind of pulse among the press, who kept asking, 'When are we going to see *The Lion King*?'" Someone else who was asking the same question was Michael Eisner.

"I don't know how we could do this," responded Schumacher to Eisner's inquiries, "except to completely explode it, and that's not what you're looking for." Eisner's response, according to Schumacher: "I don't care how you do it, just do it!"

"You know, having come from the theater, and having had my entire training and background in the theater," says Schneider, "I was very scared when the idea of trans-

 Living Lions Far Off Broadway: Staging The Lion King *in the Disney Parks*

The popular characters of *The Lion King* film naturally (and immediately) became fixtures at the Disney parks worldwide. Timon and Rafiki showed up as popular costumed characters, greeting guests and having their photos taken.

At Disneyland Park in Anaheim, a storytelling parade called The Lion King Celebration ran from 1994 to 1997. It presented the tale of Simba in the form of an African legend that's been passed down for generations. Six floats were designed around various regions and landscapes of Africa; dancers dressed in a variety of colorful animal costumes preceded a Pride Rock float featuring Simba at the very end.

The animated film and the music of Elton John and Tim Rice inspired an elaborate live show, Festival of the Lion King, that was performed at Disney's Animal Kingdom at Walt Disney World Resort in Orlando from 1998 to 2014, and in Adventureland at Hong Kong Disneyland Park beginning in 2005. Festival of the Lion King was presented as a traveling celebration, hosted by Simba, Timon, and their friends, including a band of human singers. Staged in the round, the energetic and colorful revue combined music, acrobatics, dance, puppetry, and elaborate mobile set pieces to bring to life an imaginative "tribal celebration" in an African savanna setting filled with lions, elephants, giraffes, birds, zebras, and gazelles.

In addition to the parades and shows, there was The Legend of *The Lion King,* the name of *two* discontinued park attractions; one was at Walt Disney World's Magic Kingdom, and the other was in the Videopolis Theatre in Discoveryland at Disneyland Paris. Although the blockbuster animated feature inspired both shows, they each had distinctive content and performance styles. The Disney World rendition (which ran from 1994 through 2002) was a proscenium stage presentation in the Fantasyland Theater that retold the story of the film using life-size puppets, dimensional stage sets, lighting effects, film projection, and in-theater special effects. The Disneyland Paris version (2004–2009) used human actors, dancers, and movement artists in stylized animal costumes and masks, along with sophisticated full-body costumed versions of many of the more prominent animated characters.

lating *The Lion King* to the stage first came up. The idea of being in charge and doing it badly was really terrifying. And whether it was a good idea or a bad idea—and we thought it was nutty at first—Tom and I were reacting to the responsibility for transforming this huge Disney property into a comparable musical, and we just didn't want to do it badly. We didn't want to do mediocre theater on Broadway, especially since that's what so much of the Broadway establishment expected."

"When we address developing any of our feature films into stage productions," says Schumacher, "we talk about the 'big idea.' Michael kept saying, 'You just need the big idea.' And I didn't have a big idea for making *The Lion King* work onstage"—until Stuart Oken, creative head of Disney Theatrical, floated a name from Schumacher's past. "Stuart had long been an admirer of Julie Taymor's work and I had actually tried to bring one of her shows to the Los Angeles Festival in 1987."

Schumacher had first heard of Taymor from Robert Marx a decade earlier, in 1985. "Rob was an NEA fellow at the time who soon went on to head the New York Public Library for the Performing Arts. He had essentially curated the theater component of the Olympic Arts Festival along with Madeline Puzo. And when I was working on the L.A. Festival I tried to book Julie's production of *Liberty's Taken*, a musical about the Revolutionary War. It was done in that visually enchanting style of hers but had only been staged at the Castle Hill Festival in Ipswich, Massachusetts.

"Unfortunately, it didn't work out for L.A.," notes Schumacher, "but I began to follow her career with enormous interest."

So Schumacher decided to approach an innovative and respected experimental theater and opera director/designer to direct *The Lion King*. "It turns out you don't have to *have* a big idea," Schumacher jokes. "You just have to *hire* someone who has one."

Schumacher called Julie Taymor to see if she would still be interested. "As it turned out," he says, "the number I had in my Rolodex from a decade earlier still worked!"

"I had spoken with Tom ten years before," says Taymor, "but I'd never met him, and I'd never seen *The Lion King* film, so I was kind of surprised that he even suggested it."

Schumacher in turn was a bit surprised Taymor didn't reject the idea out of hand. Why? Not only was Taymor associated with opera and somewhat rarefied original theater productions, she was a certified highbrow—and had been awarded a MacArthur Foundation Fellowship, also known as a "genius grant," in 1991. Could she produce a commercial hit with Disney material? A certain inherent playfulness in Taymor's work and its inventive visual charm suggested to Schumacher that she could.

Taymor was intrigued. "I thought, I'm not famous, I don't have a big commercial hit," she says, "so clearly if they want me, it's for something I have to offer. I would have been suspicious if they had said they didn't want me to bring my style to the project."

My first reaction when I heard it was going to Broadway was that they were mad. I could not imagine how they would do it. I was a bit worried it would look like *Cats*—but with *bigger* cats.

 **Tim Rice,** *Lyricist*

I had a vision that the characters would be like NFL mascots with furry costumes and gigantic heads.

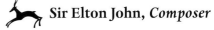 **Sir Elton John,** *Composer*

Schumacher sent Taymor a copy of the movie on videocassette (the latest technology at the time), as well as the soundtrack to the movie and the "sequel" to the soundtrack, an album called *Rhythm of the Pride Lands*, which was released in 1995. It featured music from the film score, plus additional songs inspired by the film, all with a particular African sound.

"I looked at the movie," remembers Taymor, "and I thought it was a very good animated film, but—more importantly—I immediately saw the challenge of it, putting inherently cinematic scenes like the Wildebeest Stampede onto a stage. The challenge of that excited me." And she was eager to expand the score in the same way that the *Pride Lands* album had.

But to Taymor there were issues with the story. "Are you asking me to just stage it, or are you also asking me to develop the story?" she asked Schumacher. And he said, "We have no idea."

Schumacher didn't even know *where* the show would

be presented. "When I asked Julie if she wanted to do *The Lion King*, I said, 'Look, Disney is in a conversation about buying Rockefeller Center. So we could do it at Radio City Music Hall. Or we could go to the Chelsea Piers, or buy a pier and mount it on the water—pretty much anything an avant-garde theater director might want to fantasize. Or we could do it as a Broadway show; you tell me.' That's how loose an idea we had at the time, because, remember, there was a real sense that we might not be able to pull this off at all."

It was, however, clear to Schumacher that Taymor had some as-yet-undefined vision for the project that he trusted. "She was excited by the music, by the setting, and by the opportunities for staging. She was challenged by the task of re-creating something that theatergoers would know by heart, but that she wanted them to *feel* again in their hearts. We urged her not to be bridled by the look of the movie and to create something wholly original from it."

ABOVE: *The dramatic Wildebeest Stampede from* The Lion King *film.*

OPPOSITE: *For transforming* The Lion King *from film to stage, Julie Taymor became the first woman ever to win a Tony Award for Best Director of a Musical.*

New Words and More Music

Taymor went to work on the story first. It lacked, she felt, an adequate "second act." At its root, the tale of Simba is that of a young prince who must face his destiny to be king. The universal, mythic paradigm of the story is told in the European tradition from Greek tragedy and early epics through medieval romances and into the psychological and post-psychological present.

It appears, too, in non-Western cultures all over the world. The youth (or prince or knight) must go through a life-threatening and life-defining challenge to mature to the point where he has earned the throne. "Certainly Simba goes away in the film," says Taymor, "and meets Timon and Pumbaa in the jungle, but has he really earned his right to be king? I knew that Simba had to go to a really dark place."

It was also clear that the film was short on female

Roger Allers, the film's codirector and musical's co-book writer.

characters and that the female characters needed more development, especially Nala. Taymor was also concerned with such matters as the opening song. "In the film, 'Circle of Life' is not sung by a character. It's sung by an offstage voice. In the theater, you can't do that," she instructs. "The song has to be sung by someone onstage." With that in mind, the role of Rafiki began to transform, from male to female, from animal to human, and became a *sangoma*, a South African shaman. Rafiki would be assigned the musical's opening number and the role of storyteller.

Schumacher introduced Taymor to two of the film's leading creative lights: codirector Roger Allers and co-screenwriter Irene Mecchi. "They had both been great to work with on the film," he remembers. "They are real team players, and they were already on staff at the studio."

"It started at lunch," remembers Mecchi. "I think it was in October of 1995. Tom said, 'I'd like you to meet a director we're thinking of working with for the stage version of *The Lion King*,' so off we all went to lunch with Don Hahn, the film's producer. We listened to what Julie had to say and basically volunteered to help her out."

"We would meet from time to time in a front of a storyboard," says Allers, "and start moving pins around and talking about what we could do with different moments. And she'd go, 'Well, maybe if there is some-thing that happens here,' and we'd say, 'Oh, yeah, we had thought something here.' And then Irene and I would just ad-lib a scene. I'd play Scar and she'd play Nala or whatever. And I remember at one point Julie said, 'You still have all of these characters in your heads. Why don't you guys write the book?' And we said OK."

"Happily for us," says Mecchi, "we work well together, which is part of the fun. Some people are better off writing in a hut in Scotland, or a garret in New York. But that's certainly not the way things are done in animated film."

"When you work with a team," says Allers," it's more like improv than sitting over a computer keyboard. You know, one person will have an idea and the other will react, and before you know it, you're playing 'let's pretend' and taking on different roles, and the energy spirals up."

"The harder part of it," says Mecchi, "is having to deal with feedback or notes. You can't be defensive, but it's always difficult when you think you've done some brilliant work and someone says, 'Oh, I don't know.'"

"But the feedback makes the work better," Allers asserts, "when you look back on the places where you were forced to go beyond what you thought was really good and see that being challenged made it better."

Irene Mecchi, the film's co-screenwriter and musical's co-book writer.

Taymor's quest for a "darker, deeper second act" took her to places no one could have predicted, which is what you get when you engage a singular artist with remarkable powers. And one of the places she went was to a proposed second act that came right out of her seemingly limitless and altogether unique imagination. Known as "the Las Vegas second act" to those who shepherded the musical from inception to completion, it never actually went past the conceptual stage, but it did help Taymor on the road to her final vision.

"Well, it gets called Las Vegas because that's an easy way to describe it, but it wasn't meant to be Las Vegas literally," explains Taymor. "I knew I had to figure out how to put animals onstage. Because the story on its surface is about animals, but the story is *really* about humans. And I just couldn't feature humans in animal suits. So, I thought, OK, the first act I inherit from the film is the first act, and we won't change that too much. But I gave myself the freedom to imagine a second act that is completely new."

Taymor imagined Simba running away from the jungle and coming to the edge of the desert and seeing lights in the distance, which then draw him in. "I think of it as a cross between Vegas, Disneyland, and a futuristic city," explains Taymor. As she conceived it, the denizens of the city were half human, half animal, with characters like Papa Croc, a paraplegic crocodile in a wheelchair who runs a nightspot filled with lounge lizards in snappy suits. In addition, there was a character named Natasha Leopard, who drove a Jaguar.

Papa Croc, the new father figure Simba found after Mufasa died, is also a fight promoter and wants Simba to become a boxer. Nala, meanwhile, arrives in this selfsame city and goes underground as a dancer in the Pussycat Lounge—and so forth.

Schneider and Schumacher, however, the producers of the show—and the major forces shaping the film—were not moved by this plotline.

"It was clear," says Taymor, "that they actually wanted to stay closer to the original story. They didn't want me to introduce new characters. But I learned a lot from the exercise. I never would have solved the human/animal thing if I hadn't gone through the process."

Now, writing the book for a Broadway musical is more than just penning the words for the acted scenes. The book writer, in concert with the director and his or her colleagues, creates the structure that contains the plot, themes, and emotional through lines of the characters. In addition, the book writer identifies places where the action should be carried by a song or a dance rather than spoken words. A book writer for a musical, in other words, is a bit of a juggler.

And, indeed, as Allers and Mecchi worked on the book with Taymor, they were folding in an enormous amount of new music. The animated *Lion King* film runs eighty-nine minutes and has five Elton John/Tim Rice songs. When *The Lion King* opened on Broadway, however, it had seventeen songs and ran more than two and a half hours.

"I think Julie's fundamental contribution," opines Peter Schneider, "was to recognize that the key to translating the film to the stage was to somehow create onstage the sense of Africa that you saw visually on the screen; and her instinct was that the key to that translation was the music."

LEFT: *The* Rhythm of the Pride Lands *CD was released in 1998.*

BELOW: *Composer Mark Mancina, the Broadway* Lion King's *music producer.*

But who would write the new music? For some of the new songs, it was clear that the production would turn again to Elton John and Tim Rice. But Taymor was less interested in adding pop songs and more focused on inserting additional African music, particularly the music from Disney's *Rhythm of the Pride Lands* album. There she found new versions of the movie's songs, songs created from orchestral themes in Hans Zimmer's Oscar-winning score, as well as altogether new songs, the majority of which had lyrics written in African languages. Most of the music for the *Pride Lands* CD had been written and produced by Zimmer, Mark Mancina, and South African singer-songwriter Lebo M.

The obvious choice to mastermind the score for the staged *Lion King* was Hans Zimmer. But when Jeffrey Katzenberg left Disney in 1994 and created DreamWorks SKG with Steven Spielberg and David Geffen, Zimmer went with Katzenberg as the new studio's music director. And Disney CEO Michael Eisner was not keen to hire anyone associated with Disney's new rival. So, Schumacher went to Mancina.

Mancina was reluctant. "I had a very successful film career happening at that time," he remembers. "I didn't want to leave that, and I'd never written a Broadway show. But I agreed to one meeting with Julie Taymor, and the first thing she said was, 'I don't want to revisit the film.

I want to write new music. I want to really explore Lebo's role, and I want to bring an organic nature to the music.'

"Her interest in the African music and the idea of being able to collaborate with Lebo again made me feel that the sky was the limit musically," adds Mancina. "And that made it really exciting."

Lebo M. (whose full name is Lebohang Morake) grew up poor in Soweto township, an all-black ghetto outside of mostly white Johannesburg in the days of apartheid, the vicious racial segregation that went into effect in South Africa shortly after World War II. Lebo was something of a prodigy, recording his first song by the time he was twelve.

But apartheid and the systemic poverty it created politicized him. He had, in fact, witnessed the 1976 student uprising against apartheid that is the subject of the musical *Sarafina!* Exiled from his country by the time he was fourteen, Lebo wound up in Los Angeles. There he was eventually hired to conduct an African choir on Zimmer's *The Power of One* film score. And it was Zimmer

Lebo M. wrote much of the African music for The Lion King.

who brought Lebo on to *The Lion King* film, and it was Lebo's voice on the soundtrack crying out in Zulu at the very beginning of *The Lion King* sunrise.

For Lebo, *The Lion King* is not only a fable, an allegory, or a human tale. It also has a deeply personal and political aspect to it from Lebo's perspective. "The story line of *The Lion King* is very similar to what I was experiencing in my life," says Lebo, who has no formal music training and writes in a free-flowing combination of three South African languages: Zulu, Setswana, and Xhosa (the "click language"). "As Simba comes back and takes over the Pride Lands," he explains, "Nelson Mandela came back and became the first black president of South Africa after twenty-seven years in prison."

The election of Mandela was in 1994, the same year *The Lion King* film was released. "Any contribution I have made to *The Lion King* is largely based on my personal life as a young man who grew up in exile, and came home as a successful professional. My work was

inspired by Mandela and his task of creating the path to a new future."

Like Mancina, Lebo had never written a Broadway musical. "Early in this process Mark and I came to New York for a meeting with Julie," Lebo remembers. "We were worried that we had no idea how to make a Broadway show. So I said, 'We should go to see all the Broadway shows so we know what this is all about.' We made it through the first act of one show. If I had watched anything more, I would have tried to be formal and to do everything based on chord structure and pretend that I knew how this thing works.

"But I need energy," Lebo continues. "The back and forth, the argument, and the debate, and someone telling me off and engaging the work. For me it was a much better process to work with great collaborators like Julie and Garth Fagan, like Mark and Joe Church, our music director. It was far more natural, far more organic. And I think it gave us a much more authentic sound."

"When you're working with Lebo, you have to be ready for him," says Mancina in agreement. "Because when he starts to work, it comes fast. If you have singers in the room with him, he just takes over. 'You do this, you do this, you do this, ready, here we go!' And you listen to it, and it's just magic."

Others joining the music department in this endeavor were music coordinator Michael Keller and a trio of orchestrators: Robert Elhai, David Metzger, and Bruce Fowler. In addition, Chris Montan, a longtime Schumacher collaborator, was involved as executive music supervisor. Montan, who was president of Disney Music Group until his recent retirement, has worked on every film and theater

Many of the Africans in the original cast had appeared on Broadway and on a U.S. tour in a South African musical called *Sarafina!* by Mbongeni Ngema (whose brother Nhlanhla was in the original *Lion King* ensemble). Lebo knew and had worked with the cast and used their voices, he says, as "a piano" on which to compose. "I knew their voices, and if I wanted to create a chord that could not be written in the Eurocentric mode of music notation, I could just give a note to my friends Lindiwe, Ntomb'khona, Ron, and Faca."

production Schumacher has handled while at Disney, as well as all of the original Menken/Ashman collaborations.

"So, Chris was there to help stitch the music together," says Schumacher. "And, of course, Julie had Elliot Goldenthal handy." Goldenthal, Taymor's life partner, is a highly regarded contemporary American composer with a long list of film-score credits, and he'd worked with her before, composing music for *Juan Darién*. By 1997, he'd already been nominated for Academy Awards for *Interview with a Vampire* and *Michael Collins*; he finally won the coveted golden statue for *Frida* in 2003. "Elliot didn't officially work on the show," notes Schumacher, "but he helped Mark Mancina and Julie on 'The Madness of King Scar,' for example, which is a substantial reworking of what Elton and Tim wrote."

Three songs by John and Rice were added to the musical's score: "The Morning Report" picks up on a line of dialogue in the film and expands it into a "patter song" for Zazu, who is joined by Mufasa and Young Simba. "Chow Down" is a menacing number for Shenzi, Banzai, and Ed, while "The Madness of King Scar" is an act two song for Scar, Zazu, the hyenas, and Nala. "The Morning Report" has the honor of being the only song written for a stage version of a Disney film that was subsequently animated and inserted into the film.

The music team also created three major new songs from the material written for *Rhythm of the Pride Lands*.

King Mufasa's majestic "They Live in You" (reprised as "He Lives in You") began life as a song Mark Mancina wrote during the making of the film but never offered for consideration. Nala's "Shadowland" is the English-language version of a Zimmer/Lebo song called "Lea Halalela" (Holy Land). "Endless Night," Adult Simba's aching song about the loss of his father and the need to pass from darkness into sunrise, was called "Lala" on *Pride Lands*, and its new lyrics were written by none other than Julie Taymor. "One by One," which opens the second act, is also a Lebo M. song. And the original Rafiki, Tsidii Le Loka, wrote music for herself for her character's mourning scene after the supposed death of Simba in the Stampede scene.

With the book and music in hand, Taymor turned her attention to the physical production.

The Languages of The Lion King

The songs in *The Lion King* feature lyrics in six languages other than English: Xhosa, Zulu, Swahili, Setswana, Sotho, and Congolese.

All the African music remains in its original language worldwide, with the exception of the first line of "One by One," which stays in English, as it was originally written by Lebo M.

"Hakuna Matata" is Swahili for "no worries" (*hakuna* = none + *matata* = worry).

Act two of The Lion King *begins with the rousing "One by One." The photo shows the original Dutch production in Scheveningen, Netherlands.*

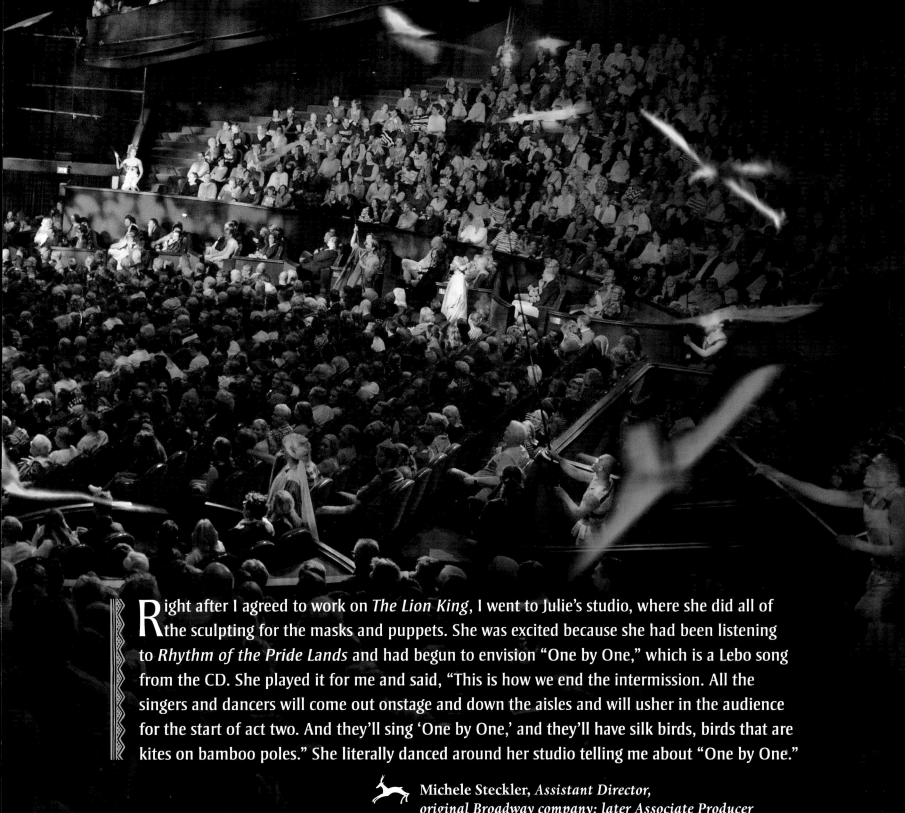

Right after I agreed to work on *The Lion King*, I went to Julie's studio, where she did all of the sculpting for the masks and puppets. She was excited because she had been listening to *Rhythm of the Pride Lands* and had begun to envision "One by One," which is a Lebo song from the CD. She played it for me and said, "This is how we end the intermission. All the singers and dancers will come out onstage and down the aisles and will usher in the audience for the start of act two. And they'll sing 'One by One,' and they'll have silk birds, birds that are kites on bamboo poles." She literally danced around her studio telling me about "One by One."

Michele Steckler, *Assistant Director,
original Broadway company; later Associate Producer*

This Julie Taymor sketch shows the animal/ human duality of the Adult Simba costume.

The Big Idea

How would Julie Taymor's vision for *The Lion King* be achieved? What physical production could match the conceptual work she and her collaborators had done on the book and the score?

"The success of the movie," says Taymor, "is its humanity. It's not that they're animals. It's that they're humans in animal guise." So, the solution to the physical production would be to visualize the animal/human equivalence. And for Taymor, whose undergraduate degree is in anthropology and who had studied theater traditions extensively in Asia, the solution was evident. She would create her characters using masks and puppets.

Masks and puppets were not new to Taymor. On a

postcollege grant, she had spent four years in Indonesia and had her own theater company of Javanese, Balinese, and Sundanese masked dancers and actors. She had also spent time in Japan and was familiar with the performance conventions of Bunraku, Noh, and Kabuki. Taymor had used virtually all manner of masks and puppets in her work and invented some of her own. It was one of the things she was known for in her world of opera and innovative theater. Taymor had also been a member of the activist Bread and Puppet Theater, where she'd manipulated the group's skyscraping puppets in outdoor productions, parades, and political demonstrations.

She had brought her ideas and concepts to the right producer. "I have a long connection to puppetry," Schumacher says. "I adored puppets as a kid and actually studied puppetry in college. I even worked as a professional puppeteer. Puppets are the ultimate theatrical metaphor."

The specific technique Taymor would employ is something she calls the "double event." You would see the actor and the character simultaneously. As in some Asian theater forms, nothing would be hidden—not the faces of the actors, nor the means by which the puppets and headpieces worked. In fact, they would be designed specifically to expose all the methods used to create the magic.

"Children have no problem seeing a doll being manipulated and believing that the doll is human," says Taymor. "We lose that as we get older. And because the story is really about human characters, I wanted the personalities of the actors to be exposed. I wanted to see their expressions. The only characters that don't clearly reveal the humans are the Tricksters, the colorful dancing characters in 'I Just Can't Wait to Be King.'"

OPPOSITE: *Taymor's character maquettes demonstrate the ingenious integration of masks, puppets, and actors.*

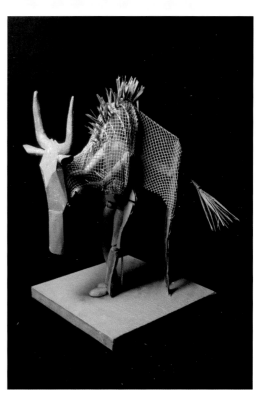

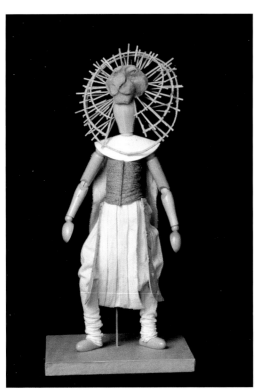

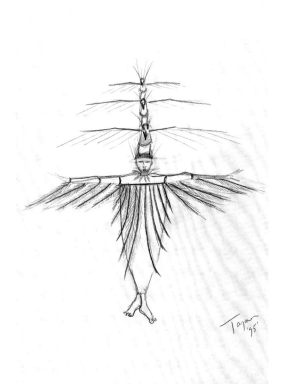

The Bird Flock costume as a sketch, a model, and brought to life by Alex Thomas in The Lion King's *first U.K. tour.*

Julie Taymor's model for the act one Gazelle Wheel and the act two version onstage in Madrid, Spain.

While Taymor worked in New York refining her ideas, Disney CEO Michael Eisner, stationed in California, grew curious about what she was up to. So, he requested a presentation of her ideas for the production design. What would she bring to the table that would transform Disney's prize animated film into a stage production of equal accomplishment? The meeting took place in January of 1996 at the Disney Institute in Orlando, on Walt Disney World property now occupied by the Saratoga Springs Resort. "I brought the sketches for the giraffes and the zebras," recalls Taymor, "and the model of the gazelle wheel."

"Michael met with Julie and Bob Crowley, whom we were considering as the set designer," remembers Schumacher. "They were there to pitch the fundamental idea of the production design. Julie brought a few pieces with her, including a small model of what we all call the gazelle wheel, an ingenious stage contraption that

looks like a half dozen leaping gazelles mounted on vintage bicycle wheels.

"And Julie says to Michael, 'If you understand this, you'll understand my version of the show. Because the dancers are going to stand in this thing and they're going to push it across the stage. And the puppets are going to rise and fall as the wheels turn. But the wheels are not going to be blocked from view, the dancers aren't going to be blocked,'" Schumacher recounts Taymor pointing out.

"Now, in traditional puppet theater you would hide the people. But she says, 'I'm going to expose all that. This is how I want to approach it. Everything is going to show. If you don't like this idea, then you don't want me.' And Michael loved it."

"Julie's presentation was so creative," remembers Eisner. "It was one of those things where you didn't have to go back and check to see what your colleagues thought. You just said yes."

And with that, all systems were go.

> When a figure made of wood and fabric moves like a living thing, the visual and emotional impact is magical. One can either focus solely on the puppet or enjoy the direct and transparent art of the actor motivating the puppet. The pleasure of watching that facsimile turn into a being with recognizable emotions is the pinnacle of this type of theater experience.

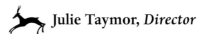 **Julie Taymor,** *Director*

The Grand Design

Taymor, who is an accomplished designer as well as director, organized the design around several key principles. For one, the underlying symbol for the show would be a circle, echoing the musical's opening song and its bedrock theme, the Circle of Life.

"As a director, you're always looking for the abstraction of the whole," she says. "For *The Lion King*, it's very simple. It's the circle, and you see it manifested in the sun, in the water hole at the beginning of act two, in Mufasa's mask, and in the way Pride Rock twists up out of the stage floor. It's all about the circle."

Also important to Taymor was that the stage version of *The Lion King* be *of* the stage. The production would be theatrical rather than cinematic—animated or live action—although there are certain images that appear in the film that trace their roots and equivalences back to the stage. Her resolve was to meet the challenges of the production with overtly theatrical solutions. There would be no apologizing when the stage could not replicate certain film techniques. The new *Lion King* would invent or reinvent techniques that are unique to the medium and as thrilling to the audience as those viewed in film. They would be different—yet they would be equally satisfying to audiences.

Richard Hudson's iconic sun is made from frayed silk on acrylic rods.

Taymor considers fabric designs for the Lioness costumes.

example, is based on a similar collar worn by the Samburu women of north-central Kenya. She also carries a fly whisk, typically made from the hair of a wildebeest's tail and carried by the tribal elders of the Maasai. The masks used in the Wildebeest Stampede scene owe their look, in part, to the widely admired masks of the Nuna people of Burkina Faso, who use their red, white, and black carvings in ritual ceremonies. Still, nothing in the show is lifted. It is all created from scratch, including the fabrics.

"It was my idea," says Taymor, "since we would not be creating literal animals for the characters, that these beautiful textiles and textures would represent the feathers or the fur of the animals."

Another guiding principle was that the Africa of *The Lion King* was not to be tied to any country or culture. It would never be the literal Africa, but an invented, visually metaphoric Africa. In fact, at the time she was preparing *The Lion King*, Taymor had never been to Africa. But by diving into her research, she found inspiration for the physical production from the landscape as well as the arts and crafts of the continent's tribal people. "It wasn't my intention to appropriate another culture," Taymor says. Her "Africa" is pieced together from multiple sources, passed through her own aesthetic, to produce the look of the show, a world of the imagination rather than a travel documentary, particularly the costumes she designed.

None of the 250 costumes, though they evoke Africa, are authentic to any country, culture, or tribe. Taymor was inspired by things like bark cloth and beading, the use of abstract symbols, and color palettes both natural and created. Still, it's possible to see specific references in the costume details. The collar of Rafiki's costume, for

Taymor's costume sketch for Sarabi.
Each of the Lioness costumes is unique.

41

Rafiki's costume evolved from Taymor's pencil sketch to a full-color rendering of the reinvented character.

OPPOSITE: *Tsidii Le Loka wearing her Rafiki costume and the mandrill-inspired makeup designed by Michael Ward.*

afiki's costume was "completed" on the morning of the first photo shoot in the autumn of 1996, when Sally Ann Parsons and I dressed Tsidii Le Loka for the photographer and realized that the transition where her "shoes" met her legs was really unattractive. OK, *ugly*—completely unresolved! We quickly cobbled together some scraps of fabric cut from the bottom of Rafiki's tunic and odd bits of raffia and wrapped them around Tsidii's ankles—and it hasn't changed to this day.

 Mary Peterson, *Associate Costume Designer, Broadway company*

PAGES 44–45: *Additional costume designs by Julie Taymor include early versions of Zazu and Timon.*

42

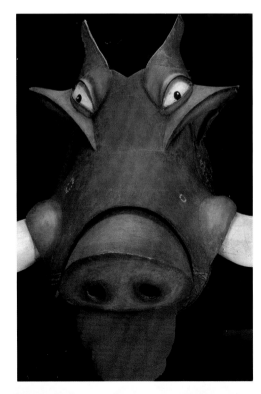
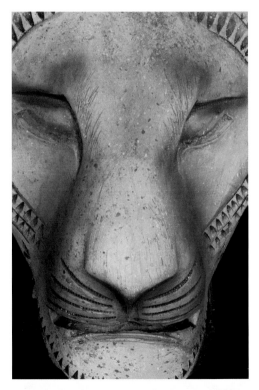

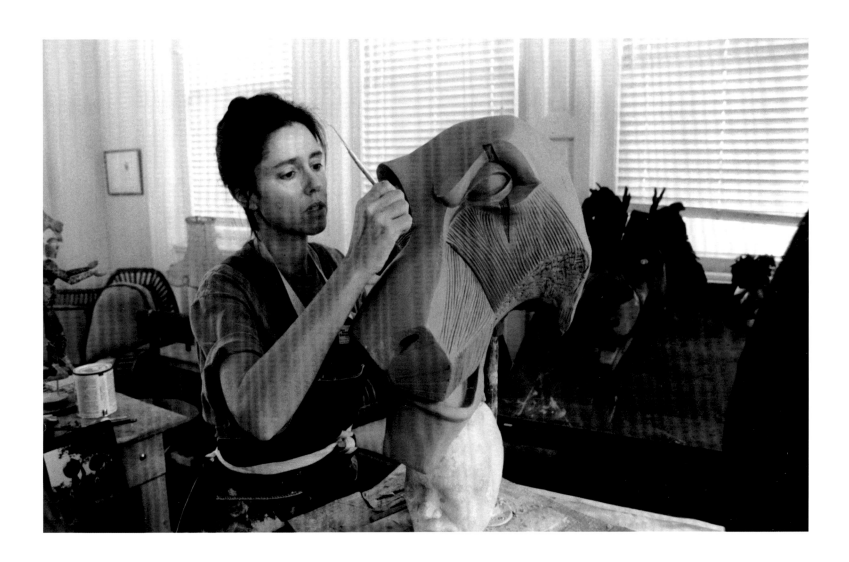

The same is true of the masks and puppets, every single one of them hand-carved and painted by Taymor. "People make a mistake," says Taymor, "when they say, 'She used Javanese puppetry, Balinese this or that.' Clearly there is inspiration from all of these different cultures and traditions, but they're used, I hope, in a fresh new way that makes them original and unique. Some of the character masks are a kind of hybrid between the look of the animation and my own style and my ideas of how I wanted the characters to be in this new piece."

To help create the masks and puppets for *The Lion King*, Taymor looked to the enormously talented Michael Curry, a unique theater artist who is known for elaborate and large-scale puppets, masks, costumes, and characters, and, quite coincidentally, had already worked for Disney. "When I was asked to do this," says Curry, "I'd already done a parade version of *The Lion King* for the Disney parks in both Anaheim and Orlando. And I had also worked on five shows with Julie, so I was very familiar with both Julie and the Disney product."

OPPOSITE: *Taymor's masks are works of sculpture.*

The focus of their collaboration, of course, would be on the animals. "We knew the big question would be where the animal ends and the human begins," Curry says. "That was the first exploration, and Disney gave us about a year and a half to experiment and make our mistakes, to explore and come up with our best solutions." What kind of mistakes? "Julie, of course, has the vision. I'm the technical guy in our partnership, and I wanted to play with lots of tricky ways in which to have the characters speak and react and reveal their personalities.

"For example, we worked very hard on an animatronic Mufasa," Curry adds. "I wanted to create a Mufasa mask that had moving eyes, moving eyebrows, an animated mouth that would react to the actor's own voice—it would be real-time animation—all the while maintaining the ability to cover the face or raise the mask, Julie's

'double event.' I spent a great deal of time making the electronics and animatronics work while maintaining the beautiful rustic aesthetic. I turned it on, had an actor put it on and speak, and knew in thirty seconds, as did Julie, that the mask was competing with the actor because all you could look at was the 'trick.' This taught us to keep things simple and allow the expression and emotion to come from the actor.

"The biggest compliment is when people say, 'I love the way that mask moves—the eyes and the expression that it gets.' But there is no movement in the mask. You're watching the actor's human face and transferring the emotion to the mask," Curry says. "And it works in that way. If you watch the actor without the mask, you get human emotion but never think of the animal. So our 'special effect' is not animatronics, it's the viewer."

Mask and puppet codesigner Michael Curry, shown with Scar, is a master of bringing inanimate objects to life.

OPPOSITE: *One of the Lioness masks.*

Costumes, Masks, and Puppets

- Actors cast in *The Lion King* portray twenty-five different kinds of animals, ranging in size from ants to elephants.

- There are over two hundred masks and puppets in *The Lion King*, including hand puppets, rod puppets, corporate puppets (multiple puppets operated by a single actor), and full-size puppets.

- It took 37,000 hours to build all the animal characters.

- Mufasa's mask weighs only eleven ounces, while Scar's mask weighs seven and Sarabi's is just four ounces. The lightweight masks are composed of silicone rubber (to form the mask imprint) with carbon graphite overlay—the same durable material used to build airplanes.

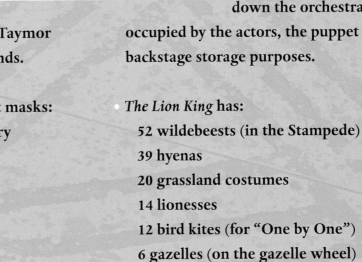

- Attached to the actor like a backpack, the Pumbaa costume is the heaviest, weighing in at forty-five pounds. The Timon puppet, which Taymor calls a "humanette," weighs fifteen pounds.

- Scar and Mufasa each wear two different masks: one moves, while the other is a stationary headdress.

- Scar uses three different walking sticks.

- Forty-five wigs are used in the show.

- There are twenty-two corsets worn in the show, each of which takes a full two days to bead.

- To maintain and upkeep the twenty grasslands headdresses on a yearly basis requires more than three thousand stalks of grass (roughly sixty pounds).

- Every ensemble member plays both a hyena and a grassland head.

- The tallest animals in the show are the four exotic giraffes from "I Just Can't Wait to Be King" that each reach a height of eighteen feet. The two giraffes in "Circle of Life" are fourteen feet tall; two actors, trained in stilt-walking, climb six-foot-tall ladders to get into their costumes for each performance.

- The largest and longest animal in the show is the mother elephant (nicknamed Bertha by the backstage crew when the show premiered in 1997). At thirteen feet long and nine feet wide, Bertha requires four actors to walk her down the orchestra aisle. When not occupied by the actors, the puppet collapses flat for backstage storage purposes.

- *The Lion King* has:
    52 wildebeests (in the Stampede)
    39 hyenas
    20 grassland costumes
    14 lionesses
    12 bird kites (for "One by One")
    6 gazelles (on the gazelle wheel)
    5 bird ladies

Sets & Lighting: More than one thousand lights are used in
The Lion King • Pride Rock rises twelve feet from out of the
stage while rotating like a carousel • The rising sun in the
"Circle of Life" sequence has a diameter of twenty-two feet.

Stage designer Bob Crowley, who had been with Julie Taymor when she presented her production ideas to Michael Eisner in Orlando—and who later designed Disney's Broadway versions of *Aida*, *Mary Poppins*, *Tarzan*, and *Aladdin*, among other projects—ultimately decided not to take on *The Lion King* before any scenic design had begun. The production team turned to another designer

familiar to London audiences: Richard Hudson. One of Britain's leading stage artisans, Hudson's credits included work with the National Theatre, the Royal Shakespeare Company, and the Royal Opera House, as well as opera companies all over Europe. He'd even done a play on Broadway, *La Bête*, in 1991, which Taymor saw.

"I was invited to New York to meet Julie," says Hudson. "I went to her apartment having only just seen the film for the first time and thinking I could not imagine how it was going to be put onstage. When I got there, I found she had started making little maquettes of the animals and carving masks, and it was so inspiring; and she talked in such a winning way that by the end of our meeting I could think, *Well, yes, actually I can see her approach working.* Then I sent a portfolio to Tom Schumacher in Burbank."

"I remember Stuart Oken bringing me Richard Hudson's portfolio," says Schumacher. "I looked at two or three of his designs and loved them so much that we

didn't need any convincing." Serendipitously, Hudson had been born in Africa, specifically in Rhodesia, now Zimbabwe, and had grown up on a farm in the middle of the bush until he was eighteen, when he moved to England to study stage design.

Once Hudson signed on to the production, he shifted his base of operations to New York for five months. "I was working at Disney's design studio on West Twenty-Seventh Street with ten assistants: five model makers and five draftsmen. Eventually we built scale models of every scene." Taymor was working in the same studio, which provided easy access for collaboration.

"I remember that we had various versions of the sunrise," says Hudson. "The early ones were almost entirely electronic, done by lighting. Then I remember one eureka moment when Julie said, 'No, I think the sun should be more like one of the puppets.' That really clicked and it became clear that the sun was going to be suspended and would rise and fall. I wanted to re-create what I remember from Africa. As the sun gets close to the horizon it appears to shimmer and shake.

"The stage sun, the object itself, is quite a delicate thing, you know," Hudson notes. "It's made of thin acrylic rods with little strips of silk with frayed edges on them. The minute it's lifted off the floor it does, in fact, start to shake."

ABOVE: *Richard Hudson won a Tony Award for his scenic designs for* The Lion King.

RIGHT: *Hudson's model for the rising sun of the show's opening number.*

There was one thing that I did on *The Lion King* for the first time that I've never done since. Richard Hudson built a series of impeccable half-inch scale models of his stage designs for some of the later presentations, and he asked me to *light* the models. The process of lighting the models in excruciating detail really expanded my thinking about how I was going to actually light the show. I made discoveries that wound up being translated onto the stage. I couldn't experiment a lot with angles, because the model box is so small. But I discovered a lot about where light should be coming from and the color that it needed to be and what worked and what didn't. It was a real revelation to me.

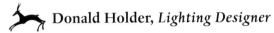 **Donald Holder,** *Lighting Designer*

Lighting design was assigned to Donald Holder, now one of Broadway's great lighting talents and an eleven-time Tony nominee. The first of those Tony nods was for Taymor's 1996 Lincoln Center production of *Juan Darién*, Holder's first musical. She loved his work and was more than comfortable working with him again. Tony Meola, already one of Broadway's go-to sound designers at the time, had provided the audio on *Juan Darién*, which

placed him, too, inside Taymor's zone of familiarity. And on Richard Hudson's recommendation, Michael Ward, whose credits included theater, opera, and film, would be brought on to design the makeup and wigs. Rounding out the design staff were associate and assistant costume designers Mary Peterson and Tracy Dorman, along with Peter Eastman as associate set designer.

Now there was a lot of work to be done.

Tony-winning lighting designer Donald Holder found lighting the set models to be an invaluable tool.

Assembling the Pieces

The first in-house presentation of *The Lion King*, an Actors' Equity–sanctioned "staged reading," took place at 890 Broadway on Sunday, August 9, 1996. A staged reading is an important step in the development of a show, a chance to put the text and the songs together in a cohesive start-to-finish manner. It gives the creative team a sense of movement, shape, and timing, and it highlights places that work and others that need further attention.

There are, however, certain union-imposed restrictions on how elaborate the readings can be. Generally speaking, sets, props, wigs, makeup, costumes, choreography, and other elements of production are prohibited, although minimal staging is allowed. Actors performing a scene typically read from music stands while the rest of the cast sits in full view. Usually there is a piano and perhaps a percussionist to accompany the songs, and someone reading the stage directions aloud. Staged readings are not for the public, but relevant individuals may attend by invitation.

On this particular Sunday, the invited guests included Michael Eisner, Disney's CEO and chairman of the board; Joe Roth, chairman of Disney Studios; and Michael Ovitz, president of The Walt Disney Company. The attendance

Richard Hudson's set model for Rafiki's Tree.

of "suits" at a presentation, particularly when it is their first exposure to a work in progress, creates an energy unlike any other, those involved in a show will tell you. Still, the cast was confident. Among them were several actors who were still with the company when it opened on Broadway: John Vickery as Scar, Tom Robbins as Pumbaa, and Tsidii Le Loka as Rafiki, along with Stanley Wayne Mathis and Kevin Cahoon as the hyenas Banzai and Ed. Keith David was drafted for the role of Mufasa. Jerry Dixon played Simba, while his partner (now husband) Mario Cantone tackled the daunting task of mastering Timon. Simone, who played Nala, later played Aida on Broadway.

The program for the day was to include the reading first, followed by a break, and then a presentation of the designs, including Richard Hudson's concept models and Julie Taymor's design sketches (as well as some of the prototype masks and puppets). "The reading went extremely well," wrote Taymor in her book *The Lion King: Pride Rock on Broadway*. "The prototype portion of the workshop, however, revealed that some of the concepts clearly worked, while others were hard to gauge in such unfinished and unrehearsed form."

Twenty years after the fact, Taymor's perspective on the event hasn't changed much: the nontheatrical people did not believe it could work. "I got the impression that Joe Roth in particular, maybe Michael Ovitz as well, thought that you couldn't put the lead actors into the kind of thing they were seeing, but you could probably use it for the chorus," says Taymor now. "The question was, 'How does the audience know where to focus?'"

Taymor was not unaware that the conditions for her first presentation were not ideal. The audience was sitting

An early version of the Mufasa mask shows off
the circle as the show's central metaphor.

too close to the actors to get any sense of the perspective a theater audience would have from a greater distance. The flat white lighting also exaggerated the mechanics of the puppets. And the rehearsal mock-ups were plain white, not artfully painted. Even she could see that some changes needed to be made.

"The masks were clearly too big. I could see that," Taymor says. "Probably a third bigger than the final versions. And Mario Cantone, who obviously hated working with the Timon puppet, made it clear that it would take someone more than four days to get the hang of working with it."

Although the reading itself had gone well, reaction to the key production strategy was disappointing. "I'm sure that if you put a movie script in front of film people and tell them that a certain scene will be shot against a green screen, they can make the imaginative leap. They know what that means," Taymor emphasizes. "They just didn't have the experience to trust that what we were doing would work."

Schumacher's memory of the aftermath of the reading is still vivid. "Because it was Sunday, there was no elevator service in the building," he recalls. "So, we had to exit down that steep and narrow stairway, and essentially, Eisner, Ovitz, and Roth cancelled the show. Michael said, 'We can't do this.

This doesn't work.' Joe Roth said, 'Everything comes down to pass/fail, and this is not a pass.' Ovitz said, '*The Lion King* is the crown jewel of the company. The show needs to look like the movie. This doesn't make any sense. No one is going to know where to look.'

"And then Michael said to Peter Schneider and me, 'You better get moving on *Aida*, because you're going to have to put something into the New Amsterdam Theatre next fall.'"

Schumacher goes on to credit coproducer Schneider with coming up with a plan to rescue *The Lion King* as Taymor envisaged it. "Peter had the vision to say, 'Julie, we failed to demonstrate the idea. So Tom and I need to go back to L.A. and present this to Michael again.'"

"I don't believe there was ever any real intention of shutting it down," says Schneider. "Things not going well, things going badly, is part of what we did. If you look at every movie we made, there was a 'going to shut it down' moment. All these great movies—*Toy Story*, *The Lion King*, *Aladdin*, *Beauty and the Beast*. At some point, we sat around and said, 'It's a disaster. Shut it down.' So my reaction was just, 'Well, we have to get back to work.' I just thought the work was too stunningly beautiful to let it go."

"I knew," says Taymor, "and Tom and Peter knew that the dimensionality of the theater allows the audience to focus on the puppet and forget the puppeteer. I believed in that completely. I believed that we would be able to do this onstage and that the audience would enjoy the art of seeing how the actor moves Timon, while believing in Timon as well."

Schumacher, Schneider, and Taymor came up with the idea of holding a second workshop, this time with the focus on a specific exploration of the mask and puppet concept and alternatives in a theatrical setting.

The Mask and Puppet Workshop

"We went to Michael and said, 'Give us a day in the theater,'" remembers Schumacher. "'We'll take three actors and have the costume shop build three different versions of Scar, three different versions of Timon, and three different versions of Zazu.

"'Julie and Michael will do three different mask and puppet treatments for each of the three characters,'" Schumacher further recalls saying, "'and demonstrate the alternatives in a performance context, in finished costumes with makeup by our designer, Michael Ward, and lit by Donald Holder.'"

Eisner agreed.

The "second workshop," as it is known now in the parlance of *The Lion King* chronicle, took place on Monday, February 10, 1997, at the Palace Theatre, where *Beauty and the Beast* was then in its fifth year.

John Vickery was back as Scar. But this time he was joined by different actors. Taking on the role of Zazu was Geoff Hoyle, while Timon was played by actor David Eigenberg (who later appeared as Cynthia Nixon's

on-again, off-again boyfriend in *Sex and the City*).

"We rehearsed for a couple of weeks," remembers Taymor. "I had come up with three different comparable versions: the 'double event' puppet/mask combination; a commedia dell'arte-inspired half mask; and just makeup. And I tried to present them as evenhandedly as possible, because I was only interested in making it work.

"I believed in the original," adds Taymor, "but I was open to another solution. I just wanted my original concept to get a fair airing among possibilities."

"It was a very long day," says Schumacher, "because

ABOVE: *Michael Curry explaining the Scar costume at* The Lion King's *second workshop.*

LEFT: *Sketches and models on display for the first workshop in August 1996.*

*Julie Taymor introduces the Ant Hill costume
at the first* Lion King *workshop.*

we had to change costumes and wigs and makeup for each of the three actors. And at the end of it, Michael decided to go with Julie's original vision."

"Eisner said, 'They all work,'" recounts Taymor, "'but your original idea is the one I want to go with. Because even though it's the biggest risk, it has the potential for the biggest payoff.'"

"And from that day forward we never looked back or asked anyone else for permission," says Schumacher.

And all that was left to do was cast the show; direct and choreograph it; orchestrate the music; build all the sets, props, costumes, masks, and puppets; and assemble it out-of-town and move it onto Broadway—*in nine months*.

Back in 1996, during the initial workshop period, I was the associate conductor, and I later played synth in the original orchestra. It was exciting to watch Julie, Mark, Lebo, Garth, and the others discover, create, experiment, play, rewrite, adjust, and define all the aspects of the eventual production. Each collaborator was striving to bring Julie's vision to life. While observing these traditional and nontraditional theatrical elements grow and develop together, it hit me that I was a part of something totally new. *The Lion King* extended the boundaries of everything I had experienced up to that point in developing Broadway shows. We were making the first "World Musical," incorporating Julie's unique storytelling concept. Wow, what a musical ride this was going to be!

 Karl Jurman, *Music Director, Broadway company*

The Casting Call of the Wild

Of the thirteen principal roles, six went to actors retained from the development process: John Vickery as Scar, Geoff Hoyle as Zazu, Tsidii Le Loka as Rafiki, Tom Alan Robbins as Pumbaa, Stanley Wayne Mathis as Banzai, and Kevin Cahoon as Ed.

"Casting is such an interesting process," says Schumacher, "because roles you think will be easy to cast turn out to be impossible. People you think you'll never get sign on happily. Our casting director, Jay Binder, brought Max Casella in to audition for Timon, and we were thrilled that he would be interested in coming to the stage." Why? "Max was in the original *Newsies* film as Racetrack Higgins, and of course had done *Doogie Howser* and a lot of other television."

Schumacher didn't think he'd get Samuel E. Wright for the role of Mufasa either. But Wright had apparently had a good experience voicing Sebastian the calypso crab in *The Little Mermaid* film, so he, too, joined the cast.

"It was very hard to find Simba and Nala," Schumacher states. The team decided on Jason Raize, who had been touring in Chris Renshaw's revival of *The King and I*, for the role of Simba. "He came to audition in L.A. and he just had something about him. I was sure right away.

"When we cast Heather Headley as Nala," he adds, "I had never met her personally because she was in Canada as Audra McDonald's cover in the out-of-town tryout of *Ragtime*. So I saw her audition on video."

Rounding out the original Broadway cast were Tracy Nicole Chapman as Shenzi and two young actors, Scott Irby-Ranniar and Kajuana Shuford, as Young Simba and Young Nala. "The last person we cast," notes Schumacher, "was a brilliant and engaging member of the ensemble named Christopher Jackson, who many years later went on to play George Washington in *Hamilton*." Jackson was also Simba's understudy and eventually took over the role from Raize. Between the New York production and the national tour, Jackson was with *The Lion King* for almost seven years.

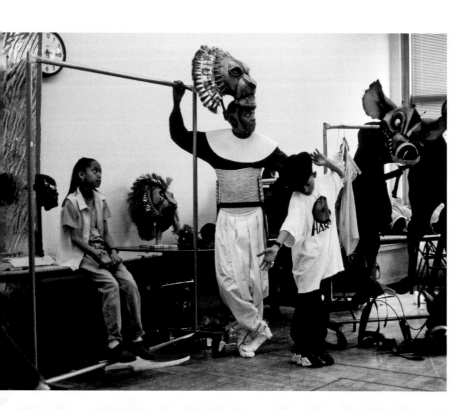

ABOVE: *Jason Raize as Simba and Heather Headley as Nala at 890 Broadway.*

LEFT: *Papa Mufasa (Samuel E. Wright) with Scott Irby-Ranniar as Young Simba and Kajuana Shuford as Young Nala.*

I had seen the movie, of course, so I went into the audition for Timon wondering how I was going to play a meerkat, and how they were going to do that. But I did the scene they gave me and sang "Hakuna Matata," and Julie Taymor said, "Can you come back at five thirty to work with the puppet?" And I said "OK, sure," but I was thinking, *What puppet? What are they talking about?*

So I go back and they strap me into this contraption they had built for Mario Cantone, who did the first workshop, and it didn't fit me, so they sort of duct-taped me into it. It was very uncomfortable. I say, "This is OK," but I'm thinking, *This is never going to work. This is ridiculous! I'm an actor. I'm not supposed to know how to do this!*

So Julie said, "OK, just move around the room. Just see whatever comes natural to you." So I'm thinking, *What am I doing?* But I keep moving, because that's what actors do, no matter how silly it feels. Eventually I started to have a bit of fun with it and started fooling around, still thinking, *There are people out there who are trained to do this kind of thing. Why don't they get one of them?*

And I don't have any trouble appearing ridiculous, but if I'm going to appear ridiculous, *I* want to be driving the ridiculous bus. The character was not nearly the challenge that figuring out the puppet was. But Julie asked me back to audition for Michael Eisner and Tom Schumacher and Peter Schneider, and they gave me the job.

—Max Casella

LEFT: *Actor Max Casella found life in the Timon puppet.*

ABOVE: *Max Casella as Timon with Scott Irby-Ranniar as Young Simba.*

Enter the Dancers

Any new production on Broadway brings out a lot of talent to audition. Furthermore, *The Lion King* would be offering a majority of its roles to people of color, a much underused group of performers, especially twenty years ago. *The Lion King* had something else going for it as well: choreography by Garth Fagan.

"I didn't want a Broadway choreographer," says Taymor. "I was looking for someone who could combine contemporary and African dance the same way the score does. The music is eclectic, so the movement should be, too. And I really liked the athleticism of Garth's work."

"Before I was ever asked to choreograph *The Lion King*, I had heard that Disney was interested in me working on one of their shows," recounts Fagan. "I was touring at the time with *Griot New York*, a collaboration with Wynton Marsalis, which features a steamy love duet with topless dancers. And I thought, *Me and Disney?* But when we were performing at the Joyce Theater in New York, I was told there were people from Disney there. And when we went to Long Beach in California and then London, there were Disney people there.

"And then a spy told me I was one of the finalists," Fagan adds. "So I thought I'd better see what *The Lion King* is about. And I fell in love with it. I had no idea how sophisticated Disney animated features had become. And I had been on five safaris and in ten African countries, so I knew I could do it. I could feel it. And then they made me an offer and I said, 'Hallelujah.'"

What Taymor may not have known was how highly respected Garth Fagan was in the dance world. The Jamaican-born modern dance master, who trained as an athlete before he discovered dance, has had a long, innovative career in a notoriously fickle field. And seven hundred dancers showed up for the show's auditions, including Aubrey Lynch II, one of several Alvin Ailey company dancers. Many were attracted more to the idea of working with Fagan than they might have been to a Disney show without him.

"Garth Fagan's name made my head light up," says Lynch. "I had worked with him at Alvin Ailey and was always a fan, because he was one of the few choreographers who was able to invent his own vocabulary of movement. Martha Graham did it. Merce Cunningham and Bill T. Jones to a degree. These are people who were able to apply their ideas to classical training and turn it on its head in a way that is instantly recognizable.

"Now, Disney and Garth Fagan are from two different worlds," Lynch goes on to note. "I had visions of furry teddy bears dancing around, but I knew that if Garth was involved, it wouldn't be like that."

The first audition for *The Lion King*, in February, was strenuous. "For better or worse, Garth decided to put his philosophy into the audition, which is you don't talk. You watch the movement and repeat what you see," Lynch adds. "He showed us a three-minute dance and said, 'Do

Garth Fagan, the Tony-winning choreographer of The Lion King.

it.' People were shocked and walking out. But I'm a concert dancer, so I'm used to that kind of craziness.

"He kept making cuts, and I kept getting called back. At the fourth audition, in April, there were only thirty of us left—and many of us had worked with Garth in the past. There were long combinations, partnering, jumping. And then he said, 'You know that first combination you did back in February? Do it.' I don't know how I remembered it, but I did. And I remember Garth and his assistant, P. J. [Norwood Pennewell], pointing at me, and me

cranking my leg as high as it would go."

Potential dancers auditioning for the show also had to demonstrate that they could sing and act, because members of the ensemble would be asked to cover the principal roles. Though Lynch was not as confident about his singing and acting skills, he was indeed cast.

Lynch soon became dance captain and eventually earned the position of associate producer, mounting the show all over the world, including the production that opened in South Africa in 2007.

The hardest part of playing Nala for me was trying to do justice to Garth Fagan's choreography. I'm still surprised he didn't kick me out of the room. I love him for that, and for all the patience he showed me. In heaven I'll be able to be a Garth Fagan dancer!

 Heather Headley, *Nala, original Broadway company*

The African Connection

From the beginning of the casting process, it was clear that the majority of the cast would be black. It was logical that a story set in Africa should be told by people of African descent, even if the characters were all animals rather than humans. In 2017, it is increasingly normal to cast a wide net to fill the roles of a Broadway musical, and Schumacher's policy at Disney Theatrical is that the cast should represent the audience. In a multiethnic urban center like New York, that means a multiethnic cast. But this was not a widespread attitude on Broadway in 1997.

Back then there were fewer precedents for a show with a black cast where blackness was not the subject of the show, as it is in *Ragtime*, or the point of the production, as in the all-black *Hello, Dolly!* starring Pearl Bailey. *The Lion King* would be the first time some members of the audience sat and watched a show with a mixed-race cast where race was not the *issue* of the experience.

Tony-nominated Samuel E. Wright as Mufasa, surrounded by the Lionesses of the original Broadway production.

For Taymor, it always seemed right that Mufasa, Simba, and Nala, who carry the dignity and gravitas of the main story, be black. Rafiki, whose character is based on the real-life *sangoma*, a shamanistic individual found in South African tribal culture, would also most likely be played by one of the South Africans in the cast. "Timon and Pumbaa," Taymor says, "are written like borscht belt comedians, so there is no reason in the world for them not to be white or black. Zazu and Scar are written with a British inflection, as they are in the film, so they could be of any race and, in fact, we went with an actor for Scar who was Caucasian as the brother of the African American actor playing Mufasa."

There was also the issue of authenticity. When it became clear that Mark Mancina, Lebo M., and the rest of the musicians on the creative staff were concocting a score with pronounced South African components, from the vocals to the instrumentation, it seemed right to seek out Africans for the cast. Lebo, for example, wanted at least half the chorus to be from Africa. There was also an issue of moral rectitude to seeking talent in South Africa. Not going to the source of the music in the South African culture seemed exploitive. So, the producers—Tom Schumacher and Peter Schneider—sought to hire Africans for as many positions as they were allowed.

Some of those actors were living in the United States and had already achieved resident status, including the right to work. Lebo M. was one such person, as was Nandi Morake, a singer who became a member of the original ensemble. But to find a significant pool of additional singers and dancers steeped in the South African musical tradition, there was only one place to look: South Africa.

But getting permission to cast the African nationals was not easy. There were the usual U.S. government hurdles to jump when seeking to employ "aliens," though if someone has a skill that is not available in the United States, a guaranteed job, and a sponsor behind them, it can usually be arranged. There was the additional issue of Actors' Equity. It is the job of the union to protect its members. While it is relatively easy to get approval for stars of shows that transfer from London to Broadway, for example, it is more difficult to bring in ensemble members and supporting players—especially on a permanent basis. Often permission is granted for a limited period, at which point the imported talent must be replaced by home-grown union members.

Negotiations ensued between Disney Theatrical and the union, which was not eager to break with their normal protocols or to set slippery-slope precedents. Still, there was considerable support for the production coming from inside Equity. Eventually the parties came to an agreement that recognized the exceptional nature of *The Lion King*, and Equity agreed that Disney could hire six African nationals on a permanent basis.

When *The Lion King* opened at the New Amsterdam Theatre, the largely African and African American cast stepped onto a stage that had once featured famed vaudevillian Bert Williams. The Bahamian American Williams, whose portrait hangs in the lobby, became the first black performer ever to join the white cast of a Broadway show as a member of the Ziegfeld Follies, which called the New Amsterdam its home from 1913 to 1927. Flo Ziegfeld made the wildly popular Williams the highest paid entertainer in the world.

Original Broadway Cast Principal Actors

Mufasa	Samuel E. Wright
Simba	Jason Raize
Nala	Heather Headley
Scar	John Vickery
Young Nala	Kajuana Shuford
Young Simba	Scott Irby-Ranniar
Zazu	Geoff Hoyle
Rafiki	Tsidii Le Loka
Timon	Max Casella
Pumbaa	Tom Alan Robbins
Shenzi	Tracy Nicole Chapman
Banzai	Stanley Wayne Mathis
Ed	Kevin Cahoon

Julie Taymor and Michael Curry rehearse with John Vickery (Scar) in New York.

Rehearse, Rehearse, and Rehearse!

The first rehearsal of *The Lion King* took place on Wednesday, May 14, 1997, at 890 Broadway in New York City. The building, which is on the corner of Nineteenth Street, was built in 1906 and was once owned by Broadway legend Michael Bennett. It is home to rehearsal halls that have been used by Broadway musicals and ballet companies for decades.

As is typical for a Disney production, the first rehearsal was attended by virtually everyone involved in the production. Introductions were made. The script was read and sung. And the designs were presented. A first rehearsal is treated like an event, a celebration, and a feeling of family begins to grow as everyone takes on their common task.

The schedule called for five weeks of rehearsal at 890 and then three weeks of technical rehearsals in Minneapolis for the out-of-town tryout, which would have its first preview on Tuesday, July 8. Given the complexity and innovation of *The Lion King*, the schedule was daunting. Conveniently, 890 Broadway was also home to Barbara Matera Ltd., one of the shops that was building Taymor's costumes. At least the endless fittings could be done on-site.

The Lion King had four main work spaces: One was for dance rehearsals with Garth Fagan. Another was set aside for music director Joe Church and Lebo M., who would also appear in the show; they worked with the chorus and soloists. The largest room was where Julie Taymor worked the acting scenes, where the rehearsal set pieces, like the Elephant Graveyard, were kept, and where all the

various elements would be put together. The fourth room was the puppet lab, which could be used for the actors with puppets to explore the "double event." In addition, it could be used for scene work conducted by Dan Fields, one of Taymor's two assistant directors.

"Rehearsals for Broadway shows are always a challenge, and ours were like a nonstop circus, almost literally," remembers Michele Steckler, the second assistant director. "We had dancers walking down the hallways on giraffe stilts and hyena legs, not to mention a large warthog and a meerkat. It became clear early on that I was the person who would always be moving from room to room to room. So I could be with Julie, I could be with Garth in dance, I could be with Lebo in music, I could be with masks and puppets."

Learning the give-and-take of working a puppet is not as easy as one might think. It was sometimes frustrating as the actors tried not to upstage their puppets, or let the

puppets upstage them. And while most Broadway musical performers are versed in three of the basic disciplines—singing, dancing, and acting—none of the cast had any experience at all with inanimate alter egos. They had to *become* professional-level puppeteers, and fast.

"Julie was great in teaching the actors how to make the puppets their friends rather than their enemies," remembers Jeff Lee, the show's original production stage manager. "She said, 'If they start to get tired or discouraged, take the puppet off. Take the mask off. Put it down. Go back to it later when you're fresh and ready to try again.'" All of which added to the strain on a rehearsal period that was barely long enough when juggling three disciplines, much less four.

"It amazes me what we did in five weeks at 890 Broadway," says Lee, who has gone on to serve as associate director on a dozen or more international productions of *The Lion King*. "In the new productions, we're working toward something we know works. In the first production, we had no idea what would work. We weren't just inventing the process, we were inventing the goal at the same time."

Scar and the Hyenas work out "Be Prepared."

Geoff Hoyle at one with his Zazu puppet.

There was another unique aspect to the rehearsals: many of the principals of the creative team had never done a Broadway musical. "Not Lebo," says Lee, "and not Mark Mancina, who was from film. Not Garth, who had spent his career in the concert dance world. Not even Julie. She'd done opera and stage shows, but never a large-scale Broadway musical.

"So we threw all these artists into a room to collaborate, and the challenge of it was none of them had ever gone through that kind of process before, so there was a learning curve," Lee explains. "Now the advantage of it was also that they had never gone through that kind of process before. So they could all come at it with a fresh notion of what it should be."

This could have had comical or disastrous results. Happily, things usually worked out. One incident in

the rehearsal period remains a classic in the minds of the company: it was the day everyone assembled in the main rehearsal space to work on "The Lioness Hunt."

"*The Lion King* was a great collaboration," says Steckler, "although it was a bit unorthodox sometimes. Now, Lebo is a great composer, but he is very 'in the moment.' He doesn't sit at a keyboard by himself. He does it in the room with the singers, because it is voices, not musical notes, that he hears in his head.

"So, the time came for Lebo and Garth to create 'The Lioness Hunt,'" Steckler continues. "And Lebo said to Garth, 'I need to see the movement or I don't know what I'm composing for.' And Garth said to Lebo, 'If I don't have the music, I can't make the dance.' But I'll never forget the day when they all came in—Lebo, Garth, Julie, the singers, and the dancers. And Garth had his dancers do some of the movement he had worked out, and Lebo was inspired and started giving the singers their parts. And before our eyes these two men created what became 'The Lioness Hunt,' one of the most memorable sequences in the show."

The Lionesses fine-tune Garth Fagan's athletic choreography.

Tom Alan Robbins getting the hang of Pumbaa.

And from that kind of interaction, the actors, singers, and dancers rehearsed, trying to realize the vision in their director's mind. However, there was only so much they could do in their space, with its ceilings far too low to accommodate major elements of the production's set. "The 890 spaces work for the usual musical theater model," says Lee. "But this wasn't going to be a usual scenario where the cast just goes from working on a flat floor to working on the actual set in the theater, where for one thing, you don't even have a flat floor, since our stage goes up and down from flat to raked. Without working on the giant set constructions—Pride Rock, the Elephant Graveyard, the Stampede—you just can't get into your body what performing the show is going to be like.

"When Michael Bennett bought that building," remembers Lee, who worked on *A Chorus Line*, "there

were two tennis courts in the basement, and that would have made a great rehearsal space for *The Lion King*. But by the time we came along, the tennis courts had been turned into a theater."

Rehearsals pushed forward until the company used up the allotted time at 890 Broadway, getting as far as they could in the imperfect space. Then on June 15, they packed their bags and moved 1,200 miles west to Minneapolis.

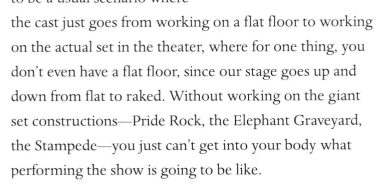

So much of Julie's theatrical vocabulary has been adopted by others that it's difficult to imagine how startling her vision was then. She had found ways to represent the characters that were somewhere between the literal and the symbolic and which allowed both the actor and the puppet to be expressive. Julie talked us through the show and the stage effects, and a year later, when we opened on Broadway, virtually everything in the production functioned exactly the way she described. *The Lion King* was fully formed in the mind of Julie Taymor on the first day of the first reading. I have no idea how she did that.

 Tom Alan Robbins, *Pumbaa, original Broadway company*

The historic Orpheum Theatre in Minneapolis.

The Lion King Meets the Midwest

The Lion King's out-of-town tryout was scheduled for the Orpheum Theatre in Minneapolis. The 1921 Broadway-style theater with 2,600 seats and three balconies had been owned by local legend Bob Dylan from 1979 to 1988 and renovated by the city in 1993.

The first preview of Disney's highly publicized new stage venture was set for Tuesday, July 8. One thing was abundantly clear: after just five weeks of rehearsal at 890 Broadway, and just three weeks to "work out the technical kinks on-site," the show was far from ready to open. The production would need all the blessings of the theater spirits to be ready in time.

But the theater spirits were in a particularly mischievous mood—and the first thing that happened in Minneapolis was that Julie Taymor, soon after checking into her hotel, had a gallstone attack so severe that she was rushed to the hospital for emergency surgery. The long, boring,

difficult, and altogether necessary process of technical rehearsals would have to start without her.

Ever the trouper, Taymor was back in the theater, minus her gallbladder, within days, recuperating on pillows on a Barcalounger recliner in the middle of the orchestra section while the tech rehearsals inched forward.

"There are aspects of the set that are very simple, that are effective *because* they are simple," says Lee, "like the shrinking pond, which is a large circular piece of blue silk that someone pulls through a hole in the stage floor. But there [are also] aspects that are far more complex. There was a lot of technology involved. There were holes opening in the floor. There were elevators, turntables, rigged decks and automated scenery, flying actors, and dancers running on- and offstage."

In addition to everything the audience would see, the company also had to choreograph the backstage traffic. And at the same time, the tech crew was learning the brand-new art of computerized stagecraft.

They were also, of course, trying to make all of it seem like magic rather than physics; essentially, to make the difficult seem easy. "I mean, Pride Rock rotates and rises at the beginning of the show," says Lee, "and we want that to be theatrical and beautiful. We don't want the audience to sit there thinking, there is a wood and steel ramp coming up out of a hole in the floor."

In actuality, the technical issues nearly overwhelmed the whole production. One problem was a faulty flying apparatus for "I Just Can't Wait to Be King," which meant rechoreographing the scene without Young Simba and Young Nala "flying" at all. There were problems with the "bug boxes," which moved across the front of the stage in the scene where Timon and Pumbaa teach Simba to eat insects. Bertha, the big elephant in the opening procession of "Circle of Life," was too big to get into the auditorium; the actress playing Sarabi was afraid of heights, which made climbing an upwardly corkscrewing Pride Rock more than a little problematic; and there was no time for the ensemble members playing hyenas in "Be Prepared" to make a lightning-quick costume change for the Wildebeest Stampede scene that followed immediately in the script.

Despite Herculean efforts across the board, there just wasn't enough time in Minneapolis to fix everything. Going into the first preview, there were still tech issues (the Pride Rock computer was proving to be unreliable), quick-change concerns, frazzled nerves, and widespread trepidation. And every single person you talk to says the same thing: no one had any idea if the show worked.

"The very first performance of *The Lion King* almost didn't happen," says Jack Eldon, Disney Theatrical's vice president of domestic touring. "The technical rehearsals were complex and painstaking, and it was difficult for the team to stay on schedule. In an effort to ensure everyone's safety, onstage and off, scenes were rehearsed over and over. But there was one point of concern for everyone involved in the production: there had been no time to run the entire show from start to finish before the first preview."

"Minneapolis was a nightmare," remembers Schumacher. "It was just one thing after another. The whole tech process was brutal. I wanted to cancel the first preview, which was only fifty percent sold, but there was a minister coming from a hundred miles away with four busloads of people, and he just freaked when we told him we might cancel. So we decided to just do it. The first time the show was ever run from beginning to end was in front of an audience."

Well, not quite from beginning to end. Before that first preview commenced, and for the week following, Schneider and Schumacher—who had shepherded both the film and this nascent musical into the world—came out onstage to address the audience. They announced, in their charmingly winning tag team way, that the show was a tryout, after all, and that there was every possibility there might be a few snafus.

They asked the audience to bear with them if something went wrong, and pointed out that there was one particularly problematic scene change in the show (after the "Be Prepared" number), and that they would take a slight pause, bring up the lights halfway for a few minutes, and continue—without an intermission.

No one knew what to expect.

> I learned two major things from Julie working with her on *Juan Darién*. One is that there is never only one way to achieve something; there are many paths to the top of a mountain. And the other thing is that she never takes no for an answer. If she can conceive of something, she believes that it can be done, so for her the collaborative process is figuring out how to get it accomplished. And that means that everyone is being pushed to their creative limit. Now, that can be infuriating and frustrating, but it can also be extremely gratifying when something impossible is accomplished and you have had something to do with that.
>
> **Jeff Lee,** *Production Stage Manager, original Broadway company; later Associate Director*

In August 1997, when I was the theater columnist for the *New York Daily News*, I went to Minneapolis to see for myself if *The Lion King* was indeed scaring children.

A columnist at a rival newspaper had written that Disney's new Broadway-bound show was more frightening than the Haunted Mansion. The columnist had a reputation for making things up, but his charge had gained currency on Broadway. And it wasn't completely off the wall. I had admired Julie Taymor's avant-garde productions, especially *Juan Darién: A Carnival Mass*. But cute, cuddly, and kiddie-friendly they weren't.

Perhaps Disney, in hiring Taymor to direct *The Lion King*, had made a mistake.

Was disaster in the offing?

I checked into my hotel on August 30, 1997. I remember the date because when I turned on CNN that night I learned that Princess Diana had been killed in a car crash in Paris.

I was due to see the show the next day, so I had a free night to kick around town. But curiosity got the better of me, and I headed over to the Orpheum Theatre just before curtain time. I love old theaters. I like to poke around stage doors, a bit like Eve Harrington in *All About Eve*.

As I walked around to the back of the Orpheum (about 8:15 or so), I heard a rumble coming through the brick wall. I wasn't sure what it was at first, so I put my ear to the wall. I heard roaring, cheering, applauding, and stomping for several minutes. Whatever was going on in there, it wasn't scaring anybody.

The next day, after a quick introduction to a couple of Disney execs I didn't know (Peter Schneider and Tom Schumacher), I settled into my aisle seat. I folded my arms, leaned back, and affected a "show me" attitude.

Out-of-town audiences are a lot easier on shows than New Yorkers. The roar I heard the night before was still ringing in my ears, but as a tough showbiz columnist, my guard was up.

Then Tsidii Le Loka as Rafiki came out and started calling back and forth to Lebo M. As she did so, a gorgeous, giant orange sun began to rise over the stage. My clenched arms loosened. The cast sang the familiar opening lines of Elton John and Tim Rice's "Circle of Life." Two giraffes loped out from stage left; a cheetah pawed the air from stage right. My arms had now dropped to my sides. The other thing that dropped was my jaw. Here was the Serengeti, teeming with life, in all its beauty and majesty.

A parade of animals marched down the aisle. I didn't know where to look. And then I felt something brush up against me. I looked up and saw a life-size elephant towering over me.

When the opening number ended, the audience was on its feet—some were standing on their seats—cheering and wiping away tears of joy.

And to my surprise, so was I, tears included.

I met Julie, Tom, and Peter the next day for an interview. One of them said, "Do you think we'll be okay?"

I tried to play it cool.

"I think you'll be just fine," I said.

That may have been the biggest understatement in the history of Broadway.

—Michael Riedel, *theater columnist,* New York Post

There were still a lot of unknowns when we got to Minneapolis. A lot of the tools Julie needed to tell the story weren't available in the rehearsal hall, so we couldn't get the sense of the full picture until everything was all in the theater. A lot of things had been tested in advance, like the lighting legs. Instead of the normal masking legs, we created these tall light boxes that extend the skyscape, and they worked beautifully. But other things—like how to reveal Mufasa's ghost and the Stampede and the Waterfall—we had ideas about what we wanted, but there was no way to work them out before we were on the set. Julie did a lot of staging in the theater, and we did a lot of lighting in real time. We tried something, it didn't work, we tried something else. It was very exciting, but stressful, because we didn't really know what we had until the first preview. Nobody had any clue whether the show worked or not.

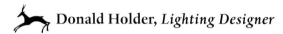 **Donald Holder,** *Lighting Designer*

But if every single member of the production team, cast, and crew was worried, their fears evaporated before the mists surrounding Pride Rock had cleared.

"So the lights went down on our first performance with an audience," remembers Schneider, "and we were exhausted. The actors were exhausted. Everybody was exhausted. And the curtain goes up and Rafiki sings and the animals come down the aisles, and the audience almost jumped out of their seats.

"They could not stop talking," Schneider says. "You could not hear the music because the audience was talking so loudly as the animals came down the aisle. And for whatever reason, there's a very visceral gut, emotional reaction to the 'Circle of Life' opening of *The Lion King*. Whatever that theatrical moment taps into, it is deep and powerful and seemingly universal."

But Schumacher now admits that he was still holding his breath. It was not until the moment after the procession that he knew the show was going to work. "For me, it was the mouse," he says. "Scar's mouse. After the biggest number of the show, we go to this tiny image of a shadow puppet in a circle of light, and the audience got it immediately. And then they got the image of the actors coming up out of the floor with the grass of the Pride Lands on their heads. They got Julie's vision instantly. It was a powerful lesson in never underestimating the audience's imagination."

"Tom asked me once when I figured out that *The Lion King* was a sensation," says Taymor, "and the answer was at the first performance in Minneapolis."

To fill the pause between "Be Prepared" and the Stampede, Taymor called on her writers to come up with a new scene to mask the scene shift and costume change. "Julie had added a short scene without dialogue, a little

Richard Hudson was fantastic to work with. I remember being out in Minneapolis getting the show ready for the first preview. And we spent an entire afternoon playing with what we call the "jungle borders" in the second act. They're stylized greenery that come out of the fly loft, and they would do everything—fly up and down, swap back and forth. And we just played, making different pictures for different scenes and figuring out the transitions from one to the next. It was so collaborative and so comfortable. He was great that way.

 Jeff Lee, *Production Stage Manager, original Broadway company; later Associate Director*

pas de deux for a giraffe and cheetah," remembers Roger Allers, "but it wasn't long enough. It took about three minutes, but the cast and crew needed more like ten."

"We needed an old-fashioned apron time filler," says Irene Mecchi, referring to a short scene that takes place in front of the main curtain while the stagehands frantically set up the next scene behind it. The scene ended up being for Mufasa and Zazu.

"It turned out to be a nice opportunity," Allers says, "to see a bit more of the relationship between Mufasa and Zazu. And it's a comic scene with Mufasa, who is always being regal, where we see him joke and play. But it's also heartfelt when he talks about Simba."

"And it's the last time you see him before the Stampede," Mecchi adds. "It was something new, it was fun as well as poignant, and everyone seemed to like it."

Thus the biggest technical problem in the show was fixed.

"We took the show as far as we could in Minneapolis," says Schumacher. "It opened, and the audience was beyond thrilled. But there wasn't any more we could do, so we just let it be. We'd make any small changes back in New York and hope that the Broadway audience would be as enthusiastic as the one in Minnesota."

The Lion King was being offered in Minneapolis as part of a season that Jujamcyn Productions was presenting at the Orpheum and State Theatres. Ticket sales to the subscribers generated about a $1.1 million *Lion King* advance, a record at the time, after which the single-ticket sales campaign went into full swing. The Disney faithful bought tickets early, but over the next few weeks, sales lagged behind our expectations. Tom Schumacher became concerned and asked our team why we thought the sales were not going well. We found that a lot of potential ticket buyers were unsure what the show was. Was it a puppet show or a furry animal show? I mentioned to Tom that Cirque du Soleil must have had the same challenge developing an audience because it was so outside the realm of a traditional circus. Tom's eyes lit up and he said, "I brought the Cirque du Soleil to the United States for the first time to appear at the Los Angeles Festival!" He and Julie Taymor then prepared a press event for five hundred of the area's top media professionals for the following week. They sat onstage and discussed the creative aspects of the show, ending the session with the celebrated "Circle of Life" processional through the theater. The press began to publish articles and photos of the costumes, which created a stunning buzz in the whole area. Ticket sales picked up to over $100,000 per day, ending in a completely sold-out run.

Mike Brand, *Executive Director, Jujamcyn Productions*

Saving Bertha

In Minneapolis, the whole opening procession was jeopardized because Bertha, as the stage crew started calling the big elephant, couldn't fit through the doors of the theater. So they figured that out, and then we were told there was no way to store the elephant backstage after the first scene. So I went to Victor Amerling, our propman, and I said, "Victor, we're going to lose the elephant?"

And he said, "Who says that?"

And I said, "Everybody says you don't know what to do with it."

"Who's saying that?"

"I don't know. I'm just told we can't have it."

And he said, "That elephant is going to be in the show."

Julie came to me and said, "What's happening with the elephant?"

And I said, "See that big huge tall guy over there? That's Victor. He is going to save Bertha."

So Julie goes over to Victor and gives him a big hug, and Victor's been a hero to her ever since. And, in fact, Victor is the propman at the New Amsterdam to this day.

—Thomas Schumacher, *President and Producer, Disney Theatrical Productions*

The Morning-After Report: Reviews from Minneapolis

"Julie Taymor's stage adaptation of Disney's most popular animated movie, getting its pre-Broadway production at the Historic Orpheum Theater in Minneapolis, is an audacious, cross-cultural re-envisioning of the film. It never tries to copy the film, the way the stage version of Disney's 'Beauty and the Beast' did before it. Yet, somehow it manages to be true to the film's spirit while becoming a playful, imaginative celebration of theater. . . . [*The Lion King* is] an evening of almost pure delight."

—Mike Steele, *Minneapolis Star Tribune*, August 1, 1997

"I would pay to see the Broadway-bound *The Lion King* again, even if I could only stay the first five minutes. The opening number, 'The Circle of Life,' is among the most spine-tingling, goosebump-raising, overwhelmingly beautiful curtain-raisers in the history of Broadway musical theater. . . . It cannot be overpraised."

—Chris Hewitt, *St. Paul Pioneer Press*, August 1, 1997

"Watching 'The Lion King' is in many ways like watching a magic act, with the audience constantly wondering what 'impossible' trick Taymor has up her sleeve next."

—Tad Simmons, *Variety*, August 5, 1997

The original Broadway ensemble joins Simba (Jason Raize) onstage at the New Amsterdam Theatre.

Back to New York

The Lion King completed its out-of-town run in Minneapolis on August 31. The first preview of the show at the New Amsterdam on Forty-Second Street was scheduled for October 15, just six extremely short weeks away for a project of this size. And the cast had the first three weeks off.

"Yes, that was really dumb," concedes Schumacher. "And I'll certainly never do that again. Our original production of *The Lion King* was not a model for how to do a Broadway show."

Luckily, as shows go, there wasn't much to change when *The Lion King* moved back to New York. "We did tons more work on *Aladdin* between Toronto and New York than we did on *The Lion King* after Minneapolis," says Schumacher.

OPPOSITE: *The fully restored New Amsterdam Theatre, Disney's home base on Broadway.*

RIGHT: *Samuel E. Wright (Mufasa) mentors Scott Irby-Ranniar (Young Simba).*

During that time the cast and the music department recorded the cast album. Some of the songs were reorchestrated. Taymor rehearsed the new material before the Stampede scene and made adjustments to the various acting scenes and dance numbers, including making some

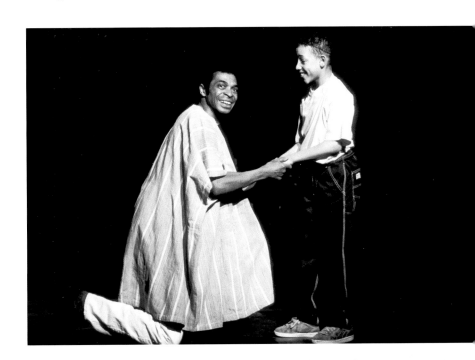

cuts to reduce the show's two-hour-and-forty-minute running time in Minneapolis. Most of the rehearsal time would be devoted to another round of tech rehearsals.

An entirely new crew would have to learn what had been taught in Minneapolis, but in a smaller space. The stage left and right wings in Minneapolis were about fifteen feet bigger than those of the New Amsterdam, and although the crew had marked off DO NOT USE spaces at the Orpheum to get the company used to what they would face in New York, some adjustments were necessary.

Fortunately, *The Lion King* was not the first show going into the New Amsterdam. The renovated theater had officially opened with a concert version of Alan Menken and Tim Rice's *King David*, which had originally been written to be performed outdoors in Israel for the three thousandth anniversary of the city of Jerusalem—a performance that unfortunately never happened. So *King David* ran for six performances on Broadway instead, and although it was far smaller than *The Lion King*, many of the details involving a brand-new theater space had been resolved before *The Lion King* set began loading in.

The original Broadway company at a tech rehearsal for the show's closing moments.

Getting the music just right was difficult. You know, when you work on a film score, you have the luxury of being able to do take after take until it's all exactly right. When someone goes to the theater, they expect the music to sound just as good, but the situation is completely different. On *Lion King*, we have a live band in a pit that has to play everything from Western orchestral instruments to African percussion to Asian woodwinds. Of course, there's a limit to the number of individuals you have in the orchestra pit, and they have to be able to play all of it. And the other big challenge was to keep the entire musical up to the standard of "Circle of Life," which is a showstopper of an opening number. It's difficult, but it's exciting, because it's organic, and it's all performed and played every single night *live*.

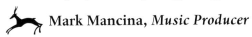 **Mark Mancina,** *Music Producer*

As October 15 drew closer, apprehension in the company increased. The reviews and the audience response in Minneapolis had been effusive and positive. But Broadway is not the Midwest. And Broadway can be skeptical, cynical, and jaded. In fact, the New York theater establishment began sniping at Disney's foray into the theater realm even before *Beauty and the Beast* ever opened. And while that show was making audiences happy, it was making the New York elite nervous. Would the Great White Way be overtaken with theme park shows and kiddie fare?

How would *The Lion King* be received?

Audience reaction during the thirty-three-performance preview run was clearly electric, and the film had created a built-in audience that produced an astonishing ticket advance stampede. But would the production find success with the help of or in spite of the press?

 ## Recording The Lion King Cast Album

We recorded the cast album of *The Lion King* at the old Sony Music Studios on West Fifty-Fourth Street, and what I remember most is that it was the most logistically fraught record I ever worked on. It was so complex, because we had multiple rooms going. When you do a cast album now, you run the band and the singers together, and you do a few takes and then you mix it quite quickly. But we had the orchestra in one room, the rhythm section in another, the choir in a third, and the principal singers in a fourth. Joe Church was conducting and Lebo was with the choir. Mark Mancina and I were in the control room with the engineers watching everything on video screens. It was just so intense, because you have one day to get all that material down, and the material itself was so complicated, both vocally and orchestrally. The African stuff was really, really detailed. I was paying attention to the lead vocals, which has always been my thing. I really monitor that part, so the next day we had the principals back to cherry out their vocals a little, to nail the details. It was also the longest postproduction I'd ever done on a soundtrack or cast album, and I've done a lot of them. Mark, our engineer Steve Kempster, and I did that in L.A., at the Village Recorder. We worked on it for a good two weeks. It was a lot of work, but I was happy with the way it came out, and it was extremely gratifying when we won the Grammy for it.

—**Chris Montan,** *Executive Music Producer*

There's a little cubby in the New Amsterdam where you can watch the show but still go mostly unseen by the audience. During our first press night, I stationed myself there. All the costumes weren't ready, every set piece wasn't in place, but we were to give journalists a little peek into the show. The theater was buzzing! Just as the lights went down, Julie Taymor walked into the cubby and we stood there together. The lights went down. The silk sun rose. The giraffes started their beautiful walk across the stage. I grabbed Julie's hands and didn't let go. I found myself crying. We both were! And right there in that cubby, I knew it: we were in the greatest show ever, and we were going to be a part of history.

 Heather Headley, *Nala, original Broadway company*

As a child of the '90s, I was always a fan of the *Lion King* film. But it wasn't until middle school, when I received the original Broadway cast recording of the show as a gift, that I really connected to the material. It was an odd time in my life, when I was just starting to contemplate the idea of mortality; that someday my parents would pass away, and so would I. This could have been a dark time for a kid that age, but I had that cast recording, and I listened to it religiously for weeks on end. The new songs added for the musical (especially "Endless Night" and "He Lives in You") really moved me. The message that your loved ones are never completely gone, and that they live on inside you, gave me a comforting feeling that everything would be okay.

 Andrew Hollenbeck, *Associate Company Manager, Broadway company*

Tony-nominated Tsidii Le Loka sings and the silk sun rises on opening night on Broadway, November 13, 1997.

PART II

FROM BROADWAY TO AMERICA

Not Just Another Opening Night

The evening of Thursday, November 13, 1997, was chilly with light rain and a moderate breeze. The southernmost lane of Forty-Second Street had been reserved for drop-offs—for guests who were attending the Broadway premiere of *The Lion King*. Many of those stepping out of their cars onto a welcoming red carpet in the theater-savvy crowd were nearly as excited about getting a glimpse of the historic New Amsterdam Theatre's $36 million renovation as they were about the show that would be opening before them. After all, prior to Disney's

own concert version of Alan Menken and Tim Rice's *King David* for six nights in May, the last live production staged here had been an unsuccessful attempt at *Othello*, starring Walter Huston, back in 1937. Sixty years of abuse and neglect later, the theater was alive again, flooded with lights and decked out in the show's boldly graphic yellow and black lion's head logo.

Elton John was there, as was his *Lion King* lyricist, Tim Rice, of course. Other invited celebrities included Julie Andrews, Mary Tyler Moore, and talk show host

Playbill's special cover for The Lion King's *opening night on Broadway. The show's logo was designed by Hans Bacher.*

Rosie O'Donnell. O'Donnell, a native New Yorker who is famously mad for Broadway, had been instrumental in publicizing *The Lion King*, inviting the cast to perform live on her hit afternoon talk show and exhorting her audience to get tickets before it was too late.

The energy inside the New Amsterdam—both in the house and backstage—was pulsating. Expectations ran high among those in the audience, and the cast was feeling the responsibility of this key moment in their lives, the life of *The Lion King*, and Disney's future on Broadway. All the years of development, the months of designing and building, and the weeks of rehearsal had come down to this performance: opening night of one of the biggest (and most expensive) musicals ever mounted, at a meticulously restored historic venue, with the direct involvement of a multinational corporation with an iconic name and reputation, careers and reputations on the line, and a guarantee of enormous attention whether the show soared or sank. It was a

killer night to be in a Broadway theater!

And the lights dimmed and went to black.

What followed next is theater legend. A tight follow spot suddenly picked up on the remarkably odd figure of a woman, who instantly cried out in an unknown language as an upstage scrim appeared. A predawn mist hovering onstage began to clear and a shimmering golden sun—silk on sticks—rose from the floor, growing larger as the stage began to fill with light. The woman—"Is it Rafiki?" many in the audience asked—who had started the show as this magical performer was joined by others; voices from all around the theater awakened until everyone was surrounded by music.

Slowly, two giraffes entered next, silhouetted against the sunrise . . . *Wait, are those really men on stilts?* And a cheetah, a cheetah that is also a dancer—that is also a puppet—entered. Soon the African chanting gave way to a familiar song, "Circle of Life," and more animals appeared, not just onstage but moving down the aisles

 *Opening Night with Mom, Dad—and Julie Andrews*

I'll never forget opening night, because I was sitting with my mom and dad, who had never been to New York. Julie Andrews was sitting near us, and I said, "Mom, that's Julie Andrews." And my mom said, "Yeah, she looks just like her." And I said, "No, it is her." And my mom said, "I don't think so." So, when we got to "He Lives in You," I kind of poked my mom and I said, "This is one of my songs." And I looked over and Julie Andrews was wiping a tear from her eye. Now for me, that's about the ultimate that I can even imagine—you know, sharing it with my mom and dad, who have seen me go through purple hair and everything else—to see them finally see that their son was finally doing something that maybe he was going to make a living by, and then being able to see someone like Julie Andrews reacting to a piece of music that I wrote. It was just amazing.

—Mark Mancina, *Music Producer*

Original Members Broadway Ensemble

Twelve singers, twelve dancers, swings, and understudies

Kevin Bailey

Eugene Barry-Hill

Kai Braithwaite

Gina Breedlove

Camille M. Brown

Iresol Cardona

Mark Allan Davis

Lindiwe Dlamini

Ntomb'khona Dlamini

Sheila Gibbs

Lana Gordon

Lindiwe Hlengwa

Tim Hunter

Christopher Jackson

Vanessa A. Jones

Jennifer Josephs

Michael Joy

Faca Kulu

Ron Kunene

Sonya Leslie

Aubrey Lynch II

Lebo M.

Philip Dorian McAdoo

Sam McKelton

Peter Anthony Moore

Nandi Morake

Nhlanhla Ngema

Karine Plantadit-Bageot

Danny Rutigliano

Levensky Smith

Ashi K. Smythe

Endalyn Taylor-Shellman

Rachel Tecora Tucker

Frank Wright II

Christine Yasunaga

Original Broadway Orchestra

Conductor: Joseph Church

Associate conductor: Karl Jurman

Wood flute soloist/flute/piccolo: David Weiss

Concertmistress: Claudia Hafer-Tondi

Violins: Francisca Mendoza, Avril Brown

Violin/viola: Ralph Farris

Cellos: Eliana Mendoza, Bruce Wang

Flute/clarinet/bass clarinet: Bob Keller

French horns: Dan Grabois, Kait Mahony, Jeff Scott

Trombone: Rock Ciccarone

Bass trombone/tuba: George Flynn

Upright and electric basses: Luico Hopper

Drums: Tommy Igoe

Guitar: Kevin Kuhn

Mallets/percussion: Valerie Dee Naranjo, Tom Brett

Percussion: Junior "Gabu" Wedderburn, Rolando Morales-Matos

Keyboard synthesizers: Ted Baker, Karl Jurman, Cynthia Kortman

Music coordinator: Michael Keller

---

of the orchestra section: there were zebras, gazelles, a hippopotamus, flocks of birds, and a mother elephant and her calf.

Then Pride Rock emerged and began to rise from the stage, spiraling its way upward and bearing characters you know as Mufasa, Sarabi, Rafiki, and the cub named Simba (a puppet in Rafiki's hand).

Ask anyone who was there that night. Ask anyone who has ever seen *The Lion King*, and few will remember an opening musical number more emotionally or aesthetically moving. When the final drumbeats of that scene echoed into the sudden darkness that followed, 1,800 members of the opening night audience on Broadway, like every audience since, burst into cheers. This was not only unlike anything *Disney* they'd ever seen—it was unlike *anything* they'd ever seen period! It was entirely new and almost overwhelming to watch.

Something entered the world that night that was unique and enormous and far bigger than the sum of its thousand parts. It was not just a hit Broadway show; it was a phenomenon—although no one knew then just how huge a phenomenon it would turn out to be. And it has only grown and spread for twenty years without a single sign of ever slowing down.

THE LION KING TIMELINE—PART TWO

1998

May 17: The 43rd Annual Drama Desk Awards; with twelve nominations, *The Lion King* wins in eight categories

June 7: The 52nd Annual Tony Awards at Radio City Music Hall; nominated for eleven Tonys, *The Lion King* takes home six awards, including Best Musical

1999

February 24: The 41st Annual Grammy Awards at the Shrine Auditorium; *The Lion King* wins for Best Musical Show Album

2000

March 23: Disney's *Aida* opens at the Palace Theatre on Broadway

June: Disney Theatrical co-president Peter Schneider leaves Disney; Thomas Schumacher becomes solo president

October 19: *The Lion King* opens at the Pantages Theatre in Los Angeles

2002

April 27: The First North American Tour, the "Gazelle company," kicks off at the Buell Theatre in Denver

November 14: *The Lion King*'s fifth anniversary on Broadway

2003

January 12: *The Lion King* closes in Los Angeles

May 3: The Second North American Tour, the "Cheetah company," kicks off in Chicago

2004

December 15: *Mary Poppins* opens at the Prince Edward Theatre in London's West End

2006

May 10: *Tarzan* opens at the Richard Rogers Theatre on Broadway

June 13: *The Lion King* transfers to the Minskoff Theatre to make room at the New Amsterdam for *Mary Poppins*

November 16: *Mary Poppins* opens at the New Amsterdam

2007

November 13: *The Lion King*'s tenth anniversary on Broadway

2008

January 10: *The Little Mermaid* opens at the Lunt-Fontanne Theatre on Broadway

March 2: The Second North American Tour of *The Lion King* wraps up in Milwaukee after nearly five years on the road

October: Disney Theatrical Productions moves into offices in the New Amsterdam space once occupied by the Rooftop Theatre

2009

April 20: *The Lion King* opens at the Mandalay Bay Resort & Casino on the Las Vegas Strip

2010

February 3: Whoopi Goldberg makes an unannounced, one-night-only appearance as Rafiki, Shenzi, and a bird lady in *The Lion King*

February 21: *The Lion King* becomes the eighth longest running show in Broadway history

2011

January 2: *The Lion King* becomes the seventh longest running show in Broadway history

December 31: *The Lion King* closes in Las Vegas

2012

March 14: *The Lion King* becomes the sixth longest running show in Broadway history

March 29: *Newsies* opens at the Nederlander Theatre on Broadway

August 15: *The Lion King* becomes the fifth longest running show in Broadway history

November 13: *The Lion King*'s fifteenth anniversary on Broadway

2013

October 20: *The Lion King* becomes the first Broadway show ever to earn $1 billion

November 30: *The Lion King* becomes the fourth longest running show in Broadway history

2014

March 20: *Aladdin* opens at the New Amsterdam on Broadway

September 3: *The Lion King*'s seven thousandth performance on Broadway

September 22: *The Lion King* becomes the top-earning title in box office history at $6.2 billion worldwide

2015

October 31: *The Lion King* becomes the third longest running show in Broadway history

2017

January 21: *The Lion King*'s eight thousandth performance on Broadway (matinee)

July 23: The First North American Tour of *The Lion King* closes in Houston after fifteen years

October 26: The Third North American Tour, the "Rafiki company," debuts at the Landmark Theatre in Syracuse, NY

November 13: *The Lion King*'s twentieth anniversary

November 14: *The Lion King* begins its twenty-first year on Broadway

Mufasa (Samuel E. Wright) and Sarabi (Gina Breedlove) look on as Rafiki (Tsidii Le Loka) shows off Baby Simba in "Circle of Life."

The entire cast and creative team take a company bow during the opening night curtain calls.

The most emotional point in *The Lion King* is the rising of the sun, the sound of the voice, and the visibility of the people in the puppets. And what that is—having experienced it all over the world, from that first day in Minneapolis, when we all just broke into tears because we couldn't believe the response of the audience—is DNA. It's in our DNA. It goes back to the very first moment that someone took an inanimate object and made it come alive, a human being making the shadow of a rabbit on the wall with his hands. Grown men, *bankers* who don't even want to go to *The Lion King*, end up crying in the first five minutes, and there's no story yet—there's not even any English.

Julie Taymor, *Director*

Opening night (from left): Roger Allers, Garth Fagan, Michael Curry, Lebo M., Elton John, Julie Taymor, Mark Mancina, Thomas Schumacher, Peter Schneider, and Tim Rice.

 Praise from the Press

"Pure exhilarating theater, unlike anything ever seen on Broadway."

—Miriam Horn, *U.S. News & World Report*

"Once every blue moon, someone takes a form of popular entertainment and transforms it into art. What Astaire did for the soft-shoe shuffle, what the Beatles did for the pop song, Disney has just done for the big Broadway spectacular. . . . In an extraordinary triumph, Taymor has bridged the gap between slick showbiz and great theater."

—Fintan O'Toole, *New York Daily News*

"Theater to roar for. From the very first minutes of The Lion King, you feel yourself on new ground—no, in a whole new world."

—David Patrick Stearns, *USA Today*

"A major Broadway event. . . . one of the most memorable, moving and original theatrical extravaganzas in years. . . . [It] is told with a theatricality that frequently takes the breath away. . . . Time and again Ms. Taymor seduces the audience into seeing what, in reality, isn't there. That is theater."

—Vincent Canby, *The New York Times*

Rosie O'Donnell offers her support.

The Lion King is the best thing I have ever seen on Broadway in my life.

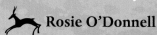 Rosie O'Donnell

"*The Lion King* is a rare theatre experience. The musical . . . is intelligent spectacle, extravagance with a purpose—and a heart. . . . The wonderment never stops."

—Michael Kuchwara, the Associated Press

"Taymor demonstrates that she's a master showman as well as a stage magician of incandescent imaginative power. . . . In *The Lion King* all the senses come together in flashpoints that can explode. . . . But it's Taymor's visual magic that's unprecedented in Broadway musicals. . . . [She] has upped the ante on the resurging American musical."

—Jack Kroll, *Newsweek*

"It's Broadway's biggest hit in years. . . . Oh, the artistry and innovation at work here—the puppetry and the visual poetry, the memorably breathtaking 'Circle of Life' opening number, the great lanky giraffes, the lovely music. . . . A special award should go to Disney for making prepubescent audiences fall in love with theater. . . . A+"

—Jess Cagle, *Entertainment Weekly*

"Wonderful. Terrific. I hope every man, woman and child sees *The Lion King*."

—Jeffrey Lyons, WNBC TV

"Disney and Broadway have found a box office bonanza that in every likelihood will run for years. . . . A stunning coup de theatre . . . unquestionably the most pulse-quickening on Broadway. . . . impressionistic and utterly graceful. . . . What should not be overshadowed by the stunning physical production and terrific score is an ensemble that ranks with the best currently on Broadway. . . .'The Lion King' is a show that will introduce a new generation of children to the theater, and doesn't sacrifice a drop of intelligence, integrity or sophistication to do it."

—Greg Evans, *Variety*

From left: Peter Schneider, Lebo M., Thomas Schumacher, and Michael Eisner.

"Awe-inspiring! Broadway theater is alive again. Taymor's imaginative ideas seem limitless. It's a gorgeous, gasp-inducing spectacle. Most important—against all odds—it has innocence. The show appeals to our primal, childlike excitement in the power of theater to make us see things afresh."

—Richard Zoglin, *Time*

"It's like being in a dream awake."

—John Lahr, *The New Yorker*

"A jaw-dropping magnificent spectacle. The show and the playhouse are enchanting. The unprecedented production is worth every penny. If this is Disney's idea of a theme park, we are delighted to report that the theme is quality."

—Linda Winer, *Newsday*

"A primal paradise . . . breathtaking beauty and scenic ingenuity. . . . You will gasp again and again at the inventive visual majesty of the show. . . . Ms. Taymor has introduced a whole new vocabulary of images to the Broadway blockbuster. . . . There is simply nothing else like it."

—Ben Brantley, *The New York Times*/WQXR Radio

"Triumphant . . . spectacular . . . brilliant. . . . It should fill the beautifully restored New Amsterdam Theatre on 42nd Street for many years. . . . visually stunning use of masks, puppetry, costumes and scenic effects."

—Frank Scheck, *Hollywood Reporter*

The Lion King clearly had fans in the media, folks who were not afraid to effuse, did not fear that Disney was going to turn Broadway into a "theme park." Were the reviews universally rapturous? No. Many seemed reluctant to overpraise the production. Many were expressing mixed sentiments, with most reviewers finding something that didn't sit right with them. But that didn't stop people from buying tickets.

"On reflection," Schumacher says, twenty years after opening night, "the reviews were not across the board glowing." Certainly, the public's affection for the massively popular animated film sold a lot of tickets prior to opening night, many of them to families with children. But that soon changed as word of mouth began to take over—in a time before instant social media reaction. "When people started to hear what *The Lion King* was," says Schumacher, "the audience quickly shifted from lots of kids to a much more traditional Broadway audience in the evenings."

When *The Lion King* woke up the morning after its triumphant opening night, it was the hottest ticket in town. At a top price of $75, Broadway's newest musical managed to bring in an unprecedented $49 million in advance sales.

There was nothing left to do but perform the show and bring the *Lion King* experience to 14,400 lucky ticket holders every eight-show week.

The arrival of the animals in "Circle of Life."

One child counted down the seconds until the 2 o'clock matinee began. A little girl stared, as did her mother, at the walls and ceiling of the New Amsterdam Theater, whose ornaments intertwined like a jungle of architectural marzipan. One evil parent turned to her son—or was it to his father?—and said, "I want you to know, a ticket to this costs as much as a ticket to Disney World for the whole day." But then the lights fell, and within moments the aisles and stage had filled with the animals of invention. Adults gasped, and every child in the audience began to reread an old, familiar text—the one inscribed on worn videos of Disney's animated "Lion King"— now brought to life by Julie Taymor on Broadway.

The special genius of Ms. Taymor's version of "The Lion King" is the way it unmasks—and de-cloys—the anthropomorphism of Disney's animated animal films. Ms. Taymor's production reveals the humans who animate the animals on stage. No actor is fully hidden by his mask or costume, and yet every actor is completely transformed by the character of animal movement. Life-size giraffes move stiffly across a symbolic savannah, but the audience is encouraged to see the human head from which the giraffe's neck rises and to admire the human frame that is poised so perfectly—so giraffely—on stilts. This is a way of articulating and closing the gap between the human and animal worlds, a gap that Disney's animation, and the often insipid philosophizing it accompanies, pretends is nonexistent.

Instead, Ms. Taymor's re-conception of the meaning of anthropomorphism reconnects the audience to the meaning of one of the signature songs in "The Lion King"—"Circle of Life." That song now not only links lions and antelopes, flesh and grass. It reminds the listener that what is human is also partly animal and what is animal is also partly human.

Ms. Taymor uses what she calls "ideograms" to represent emotion and elements of the natural world. She and her collaborators have Africanized "The Lion King" visually and musically, turning what was a piece of largely unlocalized fluff into a striking evocation of place. She has made Rafiki, the male baboon-shaman in the film, into a half-cracked, all-wise woman who wears the totemic markings of a baboon. These choices demonstrate the agility and imagination of Ms. Taymor and her colleagues. But they also demonstrate something even more striking—the Walt Disney Company's willingness, in this case, to reinvent a known, and fabulously profitable, product, not by dumbing it down to live action, as in the stage production of "Beauty and the Beast," but by allowing Ms. Taymor to test the limits of representation and theatricality.

There is no formula to be found in the way Ms. Taymor has adapted "The Lion King." But perhaps there is a useful formula in Disney's decision to use its profits to restore the New Amsterdam Theater and to unleash Ms. Taymor. There are days when the new Times Square looks like nothing so much as a grand canyon of international icons staring at one another across a river of humans far below. What a miracle it would be if the corporations those icons represent were to conclude, as Disney in this one case has, that commercial prosperity licenses—even obliges—cultural risk.

—*December 7, 1997*

THE SONGS OF

Charlotte Hlahatse as Rafiki in Mexico City.

THE LION KING

CIRCLE OF LIFE WITH NANTS' INGONYAMA

RAFIKI & THE ENSEMBLE

Music by Elton John, Lyrics by Tim Rice
with "Nants' Ingonyama" by Hans Zimmer and Lebo M.

The iconic version of "Circle of Life" that appears in *The Lion King* film, featuring singer Carmen Tillie as well as Lebo M., is a far cry from Elton John's original demo. Changes in the story's structure and details in the course of production required multiple changes. To this day, it is Elton John's favorite song from the score and the one he thought, rightly, would be the signature number of the film. The opening call of the chant, written by Hans Zimmer and Lebo M., *"Nants' ingonyama bakithi baba,"* translates as "Here comes the lion, my people, the father of our nation." "Circle of Life" was one of three songs from the movie nominated for an Academy Award.

LEFT: *Tshidi Manye as Rafiki on the first North American tour of* The Lion King. ABOVE: *São Paulo, Brazil.*

Pride Rock on the first tour of the United Kingdom.

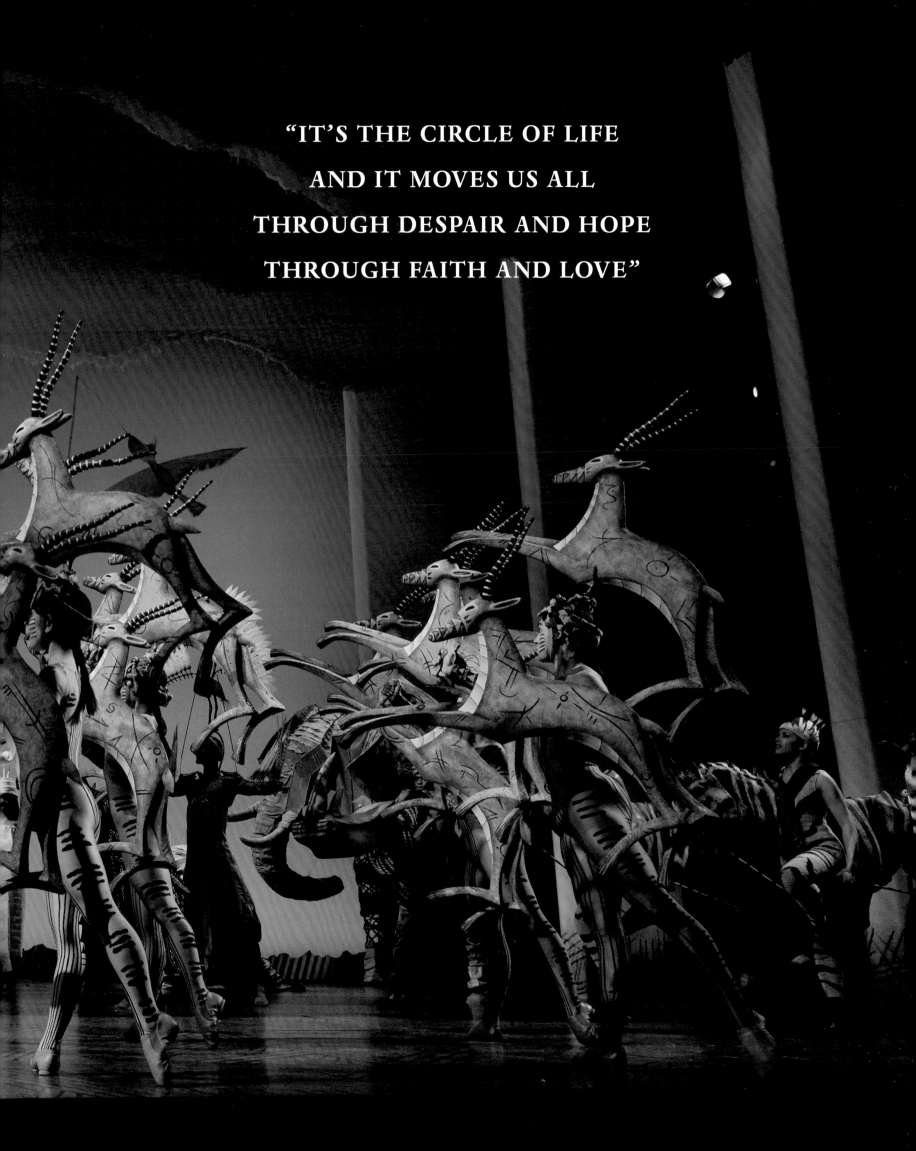

"IT'S THE CIRCLE OF LIFE
AND IT MOVES US ALL
THROUGH DESPAIR AND HOPE
THROUGH FAITH AND LOVE"

GRASSLANDS CHANT

THE ENSEMBLE

Music and Vocal Score by Lebo M.

One of the most remarkable visuals of *The Lion King* is the moment when the singers and and dancers rise from the stage with large sections of grass worn on their heads, portraying the grasslands themselves. The scene needed new music, which was provided by Lebo M. This chant, like others in the show, is sung in its original language since Taymor feels that the poetry and mystery of the original is more important than knowing what the song says.

BUSA

THE ENSEMBLE

Music and Lyrics by Lebo M.

The "Grasslands Chant" segues immediately into "Busa" as Mufasa and Young Simba enter through the grass, setting up the scene where Mufasa shows Young Simba his future realm. Kept quite simple for the musical staging, "Busa" also exists in a more elaborate version on *Rhythm of the Pride Lands*.

RIGHT: *David Goncalves as Mufasa and Tevin Themen as Simba, Scheveningen, Netherlands.*

"OH, MAMA
(MOTHER AFRICA
HER LAND AND SPIRITS)
COME, FELLOW ANIMALS!"

"RULE THIS LAND
RULE THIS LAND
RULE THIS LAND OF OURS
RULE WITH PEACE"

*Mufasa (Cleveland Cathnott) and Zazu
(Meilyr Sion) in the U.K. tour.*

> "CHIMPS ARE GOING APE,
> GIRAFFES REMAIN ABOVE IT ALL
>
> ELEPHANTS REMEMBER,
> THOUGH JUST WHAT I CAN'T RECALL
>
> CROCODILES ARE SNAPPING UP
> FRESH OFFERS FROM THE BANKS
>
> SHOWED INTEREST IN MY NEST EGG
> BUT I QUICKLY SAID 'NO THANKS!'"

THE MORNING REPORT

ZAZU, YOUNG SIMBA & MUFASA

Music by Elton John, Lyrics by Tim Rice

In developing the stage musical of *The Lion King*, much additional music was required, so the creative team expanded the score and added several new songs. One new Elton John/Tim Rice number, called "The Morning Report," is sung by Zazu, Mufasa's majordomo, and delivers fast-paced information about the state of the Pride Lands. The song is then picked up by Simba, who turns it around and uses it to mock the pompous Zazu.

Mark Mancina calls it "Gilbert and Sullivan-ish" and an especially fun challenge to fit into the musical feel of the Pride Lands. The song was appreciated for its comic value and energy, plus it expanded the character of Zazu and further defined Mufasa's role as king, although even Sir Elton admits that the song is hard to sing because the abundant lyrics are tricky.

For a special extended sequence for the 2002 Platinum DVD edition of *The Lion King*, "The Morning Report" was newly recorded and fully animated, then placed into the continuity of the animated feature. Jeff Bennett performed the vocals for Zazu, James Earl Jones reprised his role as Mufasa, and a young performer, Evan Saucedo, gave his all to the role of Young Simba.

In 2010, as the run of *The Lion King* progressed on Broadway, the show was streamlined, and "The Morning Report" was removed from the show. Other trims and adjustments included significant cuts to "The Madness of King Scar" and the elimination of a chorus from "Chow Down."

"We always felt that the show was running a little long," says Thomas Schumacher. "'The Morning Report' felt a bit like filler, like we were ready to get on with it, and it comes shortly before 'I Just Can't Wait to Be King,' so it was two songs in very close proximity for Young Simba. It's also complicated to rehearse, which takes time away from some of the more pressing scenes."

"The Morning Report" was not included in the animated feature when it was rereleased to theaters in 3-D in 2011, nor was it offered in the DVD Diamond Edition released that same year.

THESE PAGES: *Hunting in Scheveningen, Netherlands.*

THE LIONESS HUNT

THE ENSEMBLE

Music and Vocal Score by Lebo M.

The hunt of the lionesses is one of Garth Fagan's major dance pieces, and the music created by Lebo M. rises to the brilliance of the choreography. The simplest of lyrics have been arranged with vocals and percussion to be one of the most memorably dramatic musical numbers in the show.

The fierce women of the U.K. tour ensemble.

"I'M GONNA BE THE MANE EVENT
LIKE NO KING WAS BEFORE
I'M BRUSHING UP ON LOOKING DOWN
I'M WORKING ON MY ROAR . . .
OH, I JUST CAN'T WAIT TO BE KING"

I JUST CAN'T WAIT TO BE KING

YOUNG SIMBA, YOUNG NALA,
ZAZU & THE ENSEMBLE

Music by Elton John, Lyrics by Tim Rice

One of the film's six songs, all of them used in the musical, "I Just Can't Wait to Be King" is Young Simba's joyous childhood fantasy of what being King of Beasts is all about. Like the film, the stage version steps outside the established visual vocabulary and enters an abstract and totally delightful, colorful world.

Philip Oakland as Ed in the U.K. tour.

CHOW DOWN

SHENZI, BANZAI & ED

Music by Elton John, Lyrics by Tim Rice

"Chow Down," a major production number for the trio of evil hyenas, steps out of the lush African and comfortable pop realms into something darker in an orchestration that leans toward heavy metal. One of the new songs by Elton John and Tim Rice, it was trimmed in 2009 when several cuts were made to the show. Now missing is a cinematic instrumental chase around the Elephant Graveyard. But the staged number is still quite menacing for Young Simba and Young Nala, who are about to become the hyenas' next meal.

"YOU BOTH BEEN INVITED
ON A DATE

TWO COURSES HANDED TO US
ON A PLATE

WE'LL HAVE YOU RAW, WON'T
BE LONG TO WAIT

SEEING YOU'RE ALREADY
TOASTY BROWN

CHOW DOWN!"

Young Nala (Abigail Ayton) and Young Simba (Jude Blake) find themselves caught between angry hyenas Ed (Philip Oakland), left, and Banzai (Daniel Norford) in the U.K. tour.

Shenzi (Ruvarashe "Riv" Ngwenya), Banzai
(Terry Yeboah), and Ed (André Jewson) cast a
hungry glance at Young Nala and Young Simba
in the second Australian tour.

Jude Blake from the first U.K. tour.

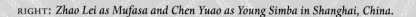

THEY LIVE IN YOU

MUFASA & THE ENSEMBLE

Music and Lyrics by Mark Mancina, Jay Rifkin & Lebo M.

"They Live in You" was written by Mark Mancina while he was working on *The Lion King* film (with Lebo M. and Jay Rifkin, among others), although he never offered it for consideration at the time. When he was asked later if he had anything he'd like to contribute to *Rhythm of the Pride Lands*, a concept sequel to the score of *The Lion King*, he took it out of his drawer. The arrangement is paired with a chant called "Mamela," the Xhosa word for *listen*.

RIGHT: *Zhao Lei as Mufasa and Chen Yuao as Young Simba in Shanghai, China.*

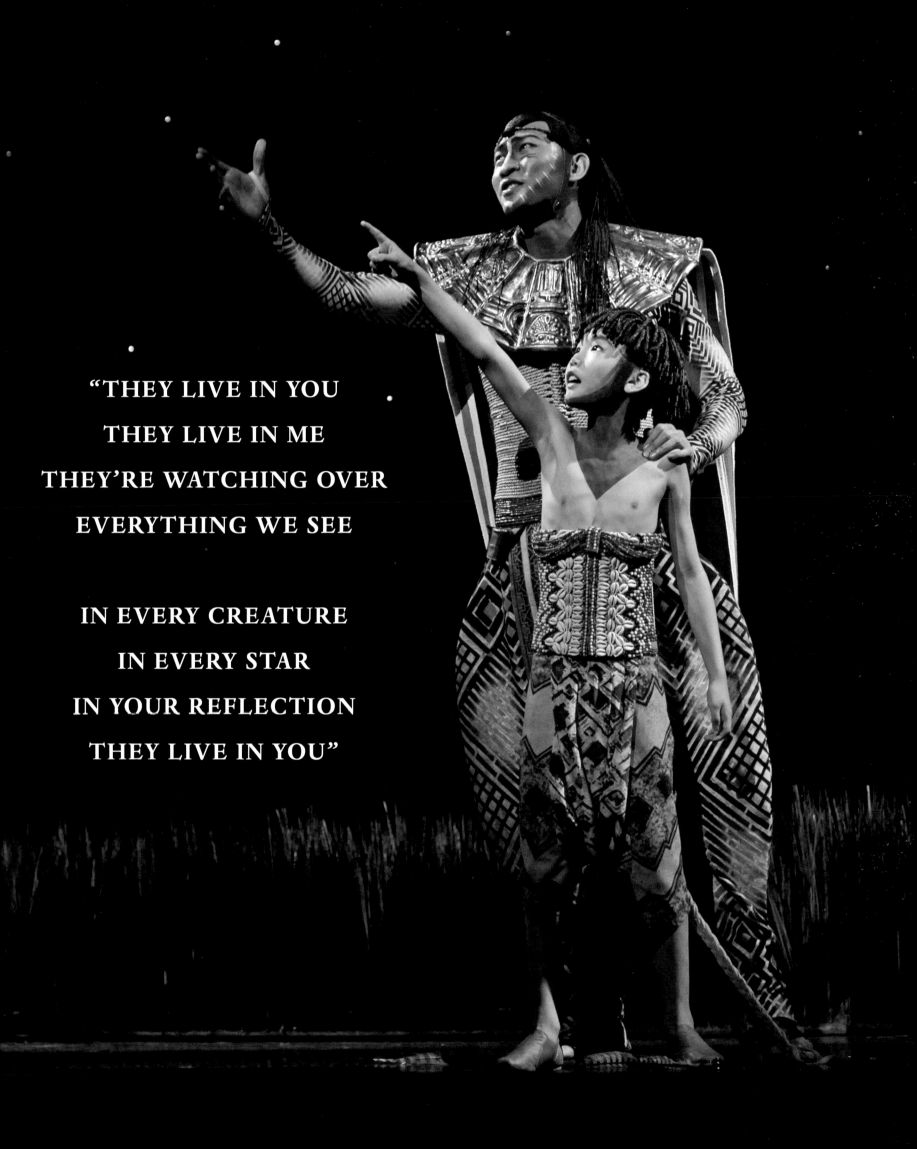

"THEY LIVE IN YOU
THEY LIVE IN ME
THEY'RE WATCHING OVER
EVERYTHING WE SEE

IN EVERY CREATURE
IN EVERY STAR
IN YOUR REFLECTION
THEY LIVE IN YOU"

"I NEVER THOUGHT HYENAS ESSENTIAL
THEY'RE CRUDE AND UNSPEAKABLY PLAIN
BUT MAYBE THEY'VE A GLIMMER OF POTENTIAL
IF ALLIED TO MY VISION AND BRAIN"

BE PREPARED

SCAR, SHENZI, BANZAI, ED & THE ENSEMBLE

Music by Elton John, Lyrics by Tim Rice

"Be Prepared," in which Scar, the villain of the tale, hatches his plan to kill both Simba and Mufasa, was written for the film and included in the musical as another major production number. The choreography features an athletic chorus of goose-stepping hyenas, but although the orchestration is full of the character's malice, the lyrics are among the wittiest Tim Rice wrote for *The Lion King*. The song also makes a cameo appearance in *The Lion King 1½*.

LEFT AND ABOVE: *Scar and Hyenas in Scheveningen, Netherlands.*

113

Scar (Stephen Carlile) enlists the Hyenas in his plot to take over the Pride Lands, U.K. tour.

THESE PAGES: *Cleveland Cathnott as Mufasa and Daniel Daszek-Green in the Stampede scene from the first U.K. tour.*

THE STAMPEDE

THE ENSEMBLE

Music by Hans Zimmer

"The Stampede" is an extraordinary piece of music written by Hans Zimmer, who won a Best Original Score Oscar for *The Lion King* film. It functions primarily as an orchestral piece in the background of the first act's climactic Wildebeest Stampede and features human voices, used almost instrumentally, although there are also a few words in Zulu. The film version runs three minutes and forty seconds; the musical's original cast album version is thirteen seconds shorter but of an equal impact that's worthy of any thriller.

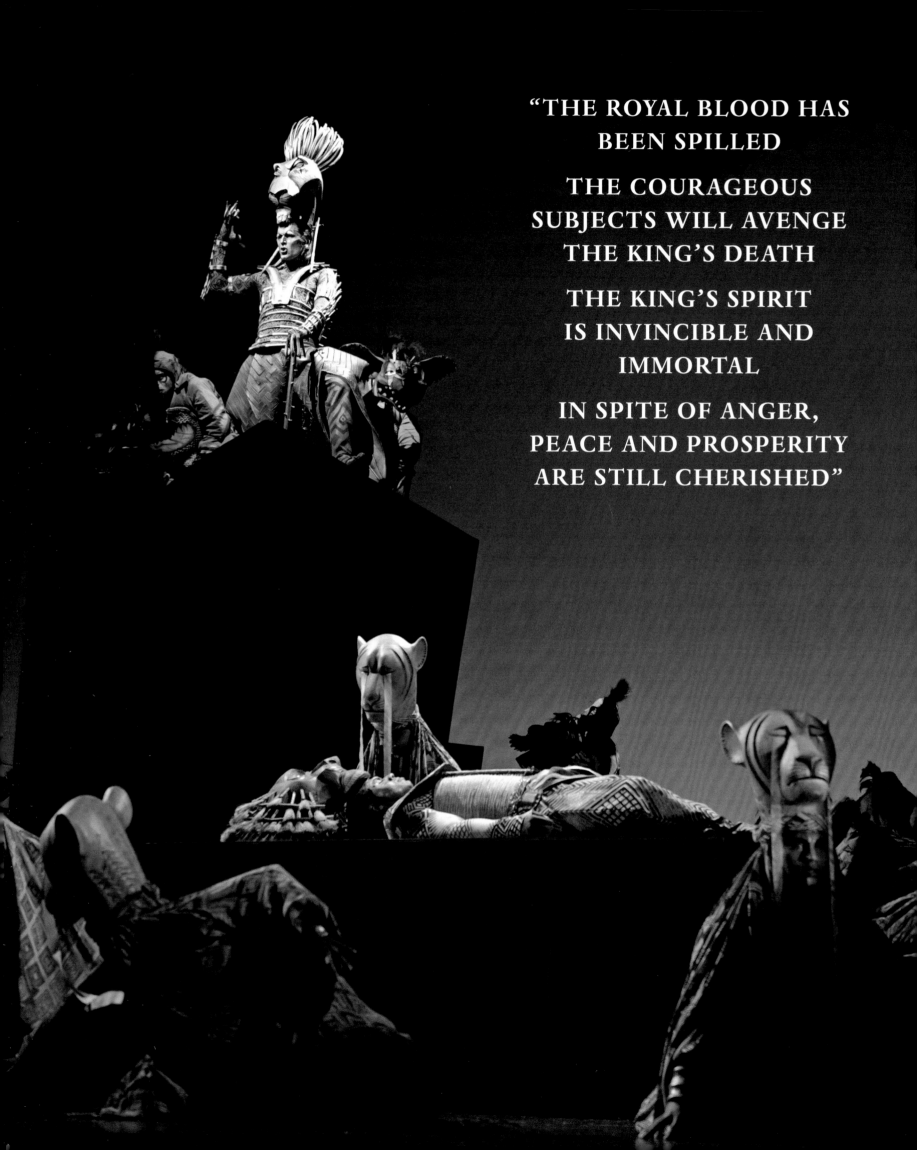

"THE ROYAL BLOOD HAS
BEEN SPILLED

THE COURAGEOUS
SUBJECTS WILL AVENGE
THE KING'S DEATH

THE KING'S SPIRIT
IS INVINCIBLE AND
IMMORTAL

IN SPITE OF ANGER,
PEACE AND PROSPERITY
ARE STILL CHERISHED"

RAFIKI MOURNS

RAFIKI & THE ENSEMBLE

**Music and vocal score by Tsidii Le Loka
with "Nao Tse Tsa" by Jacques Loubelo**

Through the rehearsal process it was clear to Julie Taymor that the stage version of *The Lion King* called for an expanded musical moment to follow the death of Mufasa and supposed death of Simba. Taymor, Mark Mancina, and Lebo M. came up with a series of three separate pieces of music. The first is a keening dirge improvised by Tsidii Le Loka, the original Broadway Rafiki, to accompany the stunning visual of the weeping Lionesses. This is followed by a short interlude where Scar reprises "Be Prepared." The final section, another sorrowful tune, "Nao Tse Tsa," which was understood by everyone to be a classic folk melody, turns out to have been the work of Congolese composer Jacques Loubelo, who would never have become part of *The Lion King*'s history had the show not enjoyed such great success.

"Nao Tse Tsa" was originally brought into the workshop room by Le Loka, who knew it from Miriam Makeba's *Sangoma* album of 1988, where it was called "Congo" and credited as traditional. Believing the folkloric tune was in the public domain, the creative team ended this key emotional sequence with a unique arrangement of the song that they and audiences found deeply affecting. Then, in 2010, thirteen years into the run of *The Lion King*, a friend of Jacques Loubelo saw a performance and recognized the tune. Loubelo soon contacted Disney, sharing the surprising news that despite being credited on recordings as a folk or traditional tune, the song was his; he even provided a copy of a 1966 film called *Kaka Yo* featuring "Nao Tse Tsa" and crediting it to Loubelo. After consulting a noted musicologist, Disney Theatrical quickly acknowledged that Loubelo should properly be recognized as a composer and lyricist for the production. He now appears in every *Lion King* program around the world.

LEFT: *Jorrit Ruijs as Scar in Scheveningen, Netherlands.*

HAKUNA MATATA

TIMON, PUMBAA, YOUNG SIMBA, & ADULT SIMBA

Music by Elton John, Lyrics by Tim Rice

"Hakuna Matata," the hit tune sung by Timon and Pumbaa while teaching Young Simba the joys of a laid-back lifestyle, was not the first song written for the film's scene. It replaced one called "Warthog Rhapsody," but not before the film cast recorded the earlier attempt. "Warthog Rhapsody" was released on the *Rhythm of the Pride Lands* CD and later rewritten as "That's All I Need" for *The Lion King 1½*. "Hakuna Matata," meanwhile, was nominated for an Academy Award for Best Original Song.

"HAKUNA MATATA—WHAT A
WONDERFUL PHRASE

HAKUNA MATATA—AIN'T NO
PASSING CRAZE

IT MEANS NO WORRIES FOR THE
REST OF YOUR DAYS

IT'S A PROBLEM-FREE PHILOSOPHY

HAKUNA MATATA"

LEFT: *Marcelo Klabin, Matheus Braga, and Ronaldo Reis in São Paulo, Brazil.*

Pumbaa (Marcelo Klabin), Adult Simba (Tiago Barbosa),
and Timon (Ronaldo Reis), São Paulo, Brazil.

ONE BY ONE

THE ENSEMBLE

Music and Lyrics by Lebo M.

"One by One" was written as an anti-Apartheid protest song, and its lyrics are frankly political. Originally sung in the spirit of "We Shall Overcome," it transformed with new lyrics from a song of angry sadness to one of victorious joy when Apartheid ended. One of Julie Taymor's earliest ideas was to open the second act with the song and to use a flock of bird kites on long bamboo poles. In every international production, "One by One" is sung in Zulu, except for the phrase "One by One," which is kept, as written, in English.

ABOVE: *Nhlanhla Ngema, Lebo M., and Faca Kulu from the original Broadway company.*

RIGHT: *The ensemble from Scheveningen, Netherlands.*

"THIS LAND OF OUR PEOPLE
OF OUR ANCESTORS AND CHILDREN
WE ARE PROUD OF IT
OH YES, MY PEOPLE
OH YES, IT'S BEAUTIFUL IN BELOVED AFRICA!"

Osvaldo Mil as Scar and Josi Lopes as Nala, São Paulo, Brazil.

"YEAH, YOU'RE OUR SAVIOR,
THANKS A BUNCH

BUT HOW ABOUT SOME LUNCH?

IT DOESN'T MATTER IF IT'S FRESH

I NEED A FIX OF FLESH"

THE MADNESS
OF KING SCAR

SCAR, ZAZU, SHENZI, BANZAI, ED & NALA

Music by Elton John, Lyrics by Tim Rice

The third of the new songs written for the musical by the film's song-writing team, "The Madness of King Scar" is a complete reworking of an earlier version originally written for the film and sung to the tune of "Be Prepared." Although "Madness" was written to fill out the portrait of Scar, it was shortened in the 2009 "trims" to the show and now barely exists in either the Broadway or foreign productions. What singing remains is actually done not by Scar at all, but by Shenzi & Banzai.

LEFT: *Barry Beijer as Zazu and Jorrit Ruijs as Scar, Scheveningen, Netherlands.*

127

SHADOWLAND

NALA, RAFIKI, & THE ENSEMBLE

Music by Hans Zimmer & Lebo M., Lyrics by Mark Mancina & Lebo M.

"Shadowland" was written in 1995 for *Rhythm of the Pride Lands*, where it was sung, in its original Setswana language, by Khululiwe Sithole, a member of the African choir for *The Lion King* film. The original title, "Lea Halalela," translates more literally to "Holy Land." Julie Taymor chose it as the signature ballad for Nala, pairing it with Simba's "Endless Night" as a way of uniting the couple musically.

Carole Stennett as Nala on tour in the United Kingdom.

The ensemble from Madrid, Spain.

"AND WHERE THE JOURNEY
MAY LEAD ME

LET YOUR PRAYERS BE MY GUIDE

I CANNOT STAY HERE, MY FAMILY,

BUT I'LL REMEMBER MY PRIDE"

Kobe van Herwegen, Steve Belmaert, and Naidjim Severina, Scheveningen, Netherlands.

THE LION SLEEPS TONIGHT

THE ENSEMBLE

Written by Hugo Peretti, George David Weiss, Luigi Creatore & Solomon Linda

Included in both the film and the musical, "The Lion Sleeps Tonight," goes back to the 1920s and its original title, "Mbube," the Zulu word for *lion*. Known in Africa via recordings by artists like Miriam Makeba, it's famous in the United States as a 1961 number one hit for The Tokens. Included in the score as a musical joke, it brings a ripple of good-humored recognition to every audience of *The Lion King*.

ENDLESS NIGHT

SIMBA & THE ENSEMBLE

Music by Lebo M., Hans Zimmer & Jay Rifkin; Lyrics by Julie Taymor

Taymor chose this ballad from the *Rhythm of the Pride Lands* album as the signature song for Simba. It was recorded as "Lala" and sung by Lebo M., who had written the original Zulu lyrics. In trying to express to her music team what she thought the lyrics should capture, Taymor realized she had such a specific idea that she should write them herself. The arrangement includes an introductory African phrase that translates as "Oh, Father! Why have you left me?"

RIGHT: *Jason Raize, the original Simba of the Broadway company.*

"YOU PROMISED YOU'D BE THERE
WHENEVER I NEEDED YOU
WHENEVER I CALL YOUR NAME
YOU'RE NOT ANYWHERE"

CAN YOU FEEL
THE LOVE TONIGHT

TIMON, PUMBAA, SIMBA, NALA & THE ENSEMBLE

Music by Elton John, Lyrics by Tim Rice

One of the original songs written for the film, "Can You Feel the Love Tonight" was, in Elton John's imagination, his contribution to a heritage of love songs in Disney animated films that goes back to "Someday My Prince Will Come" in *Snow White*. Ironically, the directors wanted to omit the song from the film, and an early cut that was shown to John had omitted it. Fortunately, Sir Elton persuaded Disney to change its mind. "Can You Feel the Love Tonight" won both a Golden Globe and an Oscar for Best Original Song and a Grammy for Best Male Pop Vocal for Elton John's end credits version of the song.

LEFT: *Carlos Rivera and Daniela Pobega, Madrid, Spain.* ABOVE: *São Paulo, Brazil.*

"CAN YOU FEEL THE LOVE TONIGHT

THE PEACE THE EVENING BRINGS

THE WORLD FOR ONCE

IN PERFECT HARMONY

WITH ALL ITS LIVING THINGS"

Hamburg, Germany

HE LIVES IN YOU

RAFIKI, SIMBA & THE ENSEMBLE

**Music and Lyrics by Mark Mancina,
Jay Rifkin & Lebo M.**

"He Lives in You" is a slightly altered version of
"They Live in You," this time sung by Rafiki at the
moment Simba sees the ghost of his father in the
starlit night sky. Rafiki reminds Simba of his father's
wisdom, of his own role, and of his need to return
to Pride Rock and claim it for the lions. The number
marks the transition of Simba from child to adult.

Naidjim Severina as Simba, Scheveningen, Netherlands.

136

Nicholas Nkuna, the first U.K. tour.

"HE LIVES IN YOU
HE WATCHES OVER
EVERYTHING WE SEE
INTO THE WATER
INTO THE TRUTH
IN YOUR REFLECTION
HE LIVES IN YOU"

KING OF PRIDE ROCK

Music by Hans Zimmer, Lyrics by Lebo M.

CIRCLE OF LIFE
(REPRISE)

THE ENSEMBLE

Music by Elton John, Lyrics by Tim Rice

After the confrontation between Simba and Scar and the battle of the lionesses and hyenas (all staged to Hans Zimmer orchestral music), Simba takes his rightful place. The the musical ends with a medley of "King of Pride Rock" (by Hans Zimmer, with African lyrics by Lebo M.); "Busa," reprised from the Grasslands scene of act 1; and "Circle of Life," bringing the score, as well as the action of the story, full circle, with the birth of Simba and Nala's cub.

ABOVE: *Nicholas Nkuna (left) and Stephen Carlile, U.K. tour.* RIGHT: *Scheveningen, Netherlands.*

"'TIL WE FIND OUR PLACE
ON THE PATH UNWINDING
IN THE CIRCLE
THE CIRCLE OF LIFE"

Awards

The Drama Desk

Spring is awards season for Broadway, and the first indication that *The Lion King* was being taken seriously by the industry came when the Drama Desk Awards nominations were announced. The group of some 150 "theater editors and/or journalists chosen for their erudition and theatrical experience" recognized *The Lion King* with twelve nominations. *Ragtime*, another outstanding Broadway musical of 1997 (which also featured a racially mixed cast) was nominated for thirteen.

At the May 17, 1998, ceremony, *The Lion King* won eight awards: Direction of a Musical, Choreography, Set Design, Costume Design, Mask & Puppet Design, Lighting Design, Sound Design, and Featured Actress in a Musical for Tsidii Le Loka. *Ragtime* took home five, including the coveted award for Outstanding Musical; it also took Best Orchestrations, plus Best Book, Best Music, and Best Lyrics—three choice categories in which *The Lion King* had not even been nominated.

Tony, Tony, Tony!

The Tony nominations were even more encouraging. They were announced on May 4 and featured a similar *Lion King* vs. *Ragtime* fight card, with *The Lion King* getting eleven nominations to *Ragtime*'s thirteen. This time, however, both shows were up for Best Musical, Best Book, Best Score, Best Orchestrations, Best Direction, and Best Choreography—as well as Scenic Design, Costume Design, and Lighting Design. Tsidii Le Loka and Samuel E. Wright were nominated for their performances; four actors were nominated from the cast of *Ragtime*.

The 52nd Annual Tony Awards ceremony took place on Sunday, June 7, 1998, at Radio City Musical Hall, the same theater where *The Lion King* film had made its debut four years earlier. Of the nine head-to-head awards battles, *Ragtime* won for book, score, and orchestrations. *The Lion King* won in all six of the other categories, including Best Musical. Julie Taymor became the first woman ever to win a Tony for directing a musical. It was a staggeringly glorious night for everyone who had ever touched or been touched by *The Lion King*.

Julie Taymor

140

We were up against *Ragtime*, and people were saying we weren't going to win a Tony because we weren't really a show. We were a kind of circus, a spectacle. But we were there at Radio City Music Hall doing what we do: we were coming together as a family, as a team, and putting our souls into everything we had learned. I remember when Tsidii Le Loka lost the Tony to Audra McDonald from *Ragtime* and some of our cast members were already beginning to cry, but we had to go on next and perform "Circle of Life." So Tsidii was furiously changing into her Rafiki costume and makeup after not winning a Tony, and we turned to each other and said, "Let's sing the heck outta this thing." I was standing in the wings with my gazelles on and Tsidii sang "Nants' ingon-yama" and we leaped. And it was just this magical experience. When we finished "Circle of Life"—*boom!* The audience stood up at once and cheered.

We had done our job. It didn't even matter what happened with the Tony Award. So, we got on the bus to go back to the New Amsterdam, and we were sad because we weren't going to win, but we were proud of ourselves anyway. We were sitting around watching the end of the show on TV, and when they announced *The Lion King* had won Best Musical, we instantly went from black-and-white to Technicolor. It was one of the most amazing moments of my dance career—that moment when they announced that all that work had paid off. And it didn't matter if we won, because we had done the work. But we won anyway! It was amazing.

—Aubrey Lynch II, *original Broadway company, later Associate Producer*

I went to Minneapolis in the summer of 1997 to see a show. Disney's *The Lion King* was in previews, and I'd been tipped off that it might be worth my time to see it. I ran a large theatrical ad agency and getting the Disney business would be a real coup. Thirty seconds in I knew it would be much more than that. Real live theatrical history was being made, and I wanted to be a part of it.

What was so clear is that the producers (the real live Peter Schneider and Tom Schumacher) had a vision and the courage to hire Julie Taymor to bring it to life. And that Julie Taymor's vision was going to do something theater rarely did: take the muscle in your mind that is your imagination and give it an exhilarating workout, leaving audiences with a new understanding of what is possible.

It was also clear that their current advertising was aiming too low. No more little yellow plastic watches with lion logos would be mailed out to Disney friends and family. This show needed to be positioned as a work of art that would win the Tony Award. It was my agency's great pleasure to get to work with a client that showed us the same trust and appreciation they showed Julie Taymor.

When we took our seats on opening night on Broadway, I was stunned. They were the best in the house: the critics' seats, the stars' seats, the theater owners' seats. Ad agency seats were twenty rows back, on the side. "Weren't Peter and Tom nice to give us these seats?" I said to my partner, Steve. "Nice and smart!" he replied. "They know you'll be selling this show for the next twenty years." And here we are.

Like it will be for the audience that sees *The Lion King* for the first time tonight, awe is the overwhelming emotion each time I see it. No tricks of technology drive the narrative, just simple storytelling with stagecraft as old as time reinvented for jaded theatergoers so that we might once again experience wonder. This is the gift that *The Lion King* gave Broadway.

Peter, Tom, and Julie—thank you from the bottom of my heart for letting me play a small part in your show.

—Nancy Coyne, *Chairman, Serino Coyne*

In September 1997, Nancy Coyne and I somehow managed to get Tom Schumacher and Peter Schneider to come up to the conference room at Serino Coyne, where the agency made a pitch to handle the advertising and marketing for *The Lion King*.

I remember that after our presentation, Tom said, "A brilliant strategy, brilliantly expressed." Peter said, "We'd like the two of you to join us for dinner." Just like that. It wasn't common in those days to get an immediate response to our work—positive or negative.

I remember that dinner turned out to include a visit to the recording session for the original Broadway cast album. There, Tom and Peter introduced us to Chris Montan and Julie Taymor as though we were old friends. Again, not common.

I remember, a month later, cutting a video montage, using news footage shot in Minneapolis, and showing it to Tom, Peter, and Julie. It was a good montage, but they acted like it had been cut by Spielberg or Scorcese.

I remember, six months after that, being taken to a theater conference in Miami—a first for me—and being introduced as part of the *Lion King* team, when the show was the hottest thing since kale—and how flattering that was.

And on that night of nights in June 1998, I remember being invited by Tom and Peter to the Tonys—another first—and sitting right behind them at Radio City Music Hall. And how—when Nathan Lane opened the Best Musical envelope and said, *"The Lion King,"* Nancy and I were right there to hug them.

I remember so many moments of that year, big and small, glamorous and gritty. But mostly, I remember those two guys at the center of it all, Tom and Peter, changing Broadway, bit by bit, day after day. The challenge of it, and the joy, and the excitement I felt at the proximity to such special brilliance; an honor and a privilege, treasured ever since.

—Rick Elice, *former Serino Coyne ad executive, author of* Jersey Boys *and* Peter and the Starcatcher

Celebrities in the Pride Lands

"Celebrities go to Broadway shows for two reasons: to see the show or to be seen at the show," recounts Dana Amendola, vice president of operations at Disney Theatrical Productions, and a member of the original restoration team of the New Amsterdam Theatre in 1995. "When Michael Jackson came to *The Lion King*, he slipped in through the side door, and left just as quietly. I don't think a dozen people knew he was there. On the other hand, when a certain ever-to-be-unnamed movie star arrived, dozens of paparazzi were already waiting for her at the street entrance. (I didn't tell them she'd be there!)

"Now, Joe DiMaggio was a huge celebrity," Amendola continues. "He was the famous Yankee Clipper of the Bronx Bombers [New York Yankees]. Joltin' Joe, as he was also called, was once the husband of Marilyn Monroe, and he was a New York icon. He made the mistake of buying tickets under his own name at the box office, and the word got out. People were in a frenzy running to the nearby sporting goods store to buy baseballs for him to autograph.

"DiMaggio got wind of it and let me know. 'I really just want to enjoy the show. I want to be part of it. For once in my life I want to sit and escape. I want this moment for me.'

"So, as the rumor spread about DiMaggio being there, I started a counter-rumor, with help from house staff, that it wasn't him at all. 'Oh, this guy. He's a well-known look-alike. DiMaggio's not here!' Several disappointed audience members went home that night having to explain why they brought home brand-new baseballs from *The Lion King*."

Who's Running This Show?

On Broadway, 147 individuals are directly involved with the daily presentation of *The Lion King*:

51 cast members	**3 sound technicians**
24 musicians	**4 props people**
19 wardrobe staff	**6 creative associates**
3 makeup artists	**5 stage managers**
2 wig/hairdressers	**2 company managers**
3 puppet craftspeople	**1 child guardian**
13 carpenters	**1 physical therapist**
10 electricians	**Together they work a combined 250,000 hours per year.**

Broadway's original Zazu, Geoff Hoyle, gets his blue on.

Be Our Guest, Our Very, Very, Very Special Guest!
When the Celebrity Runs a Country
By Dana Amendola

Bill and Hillary Clinton

In September of 1998, President Clinton and First Lady Hillary Clinton came to *The Lion King* at the New Amsterdam for a Democratic National Committee fundraiser in the midst of the scandal that preceded his impeachment trial. Clinton was under siege by the press, but he quickly found solace in the positive reaction from the audience, no more so than in act two, where Rafiki clocks Simba in the head and says, "Yes, the past can hurt. You can run from it, or learn from it." The line seemed so apropos that the crowd broke into a spontaneous ovation. At the end of the show, the orchestra added "Hail to the Chief" to the play-out music. Their mood and energy buoyed by the show and the support they felt from the audience, the Clintons remained after the performance and went backstage, where they stayed for a long time, visiting, chatting, and taking pictures with everyone from the cast to the backstage and front-of-house crew. There was so much positive energy around the event that it made the front page of *The New York Times* the next day—above the fold.

George H. W. Bush

President Clinton's predecessor, George H. W. Bush, arrived quietly at the New Amsterdam—well, as quietly as one can with a Secret Service entourage. Still, he went largely unrecognized. As I checked on him, he said, "I can't tell you how happy I am to just sit quietly and enjoy this show." Typically, VIPs, and especially world leaders,

leave the show a bit early, a practice necessitated by security logistics. Former president Bush wouldn't leave early. He stayed to the very end, and seemed to be completely transported by the whole experience.

Mikhail Gorbachev

Former General Secretary of the Communist Party of the Soviet Union

The leader of the "Evil Empire," as President Ronald Reagan dubbed the USSR in 1983, also came to *The Lion King*. As a Cold War kid, this was a little startling to me. He and the Soviet Union had been the enemy of our way of life, and here I was assigned to escort him and his entourage. I was pleasantly surprised at his joviality. He was simply over the moon to be there and was delighted to be taken backstage to see the puppetry and stagecraft. I asked through his translator if he'd like to meet the cast. He was ecstatic.

As the call went out to the cast, I realized that most of them were too young to fully understand who Gorbachev was. But at the time, he was appearing in an international TV ad for Pizza Hut (no kidding, check YouTube). And one young dancer tore down to the stage, wanting to get a picture with "the Pizza Hut dude!"

"*Da! Da!* Pizza Hut! Pizza Hut!" Gorbachev responded. "Everyone love Pizza Hut!"

Benjamin Netanyahu

Prime Minister of Israel

Dignitaries typically will secure tickets through their security service so the bodyguards can all get tickets in a protective position (usually the two seats behind the

official). Prime Minister Netanyahu purchased his tickets through our publicity agent, which did not suit the Mossad (Israel's equivalent of our Secret Service). Upon arrival—five minutes before the curtain—they made a firm request that Netanyahu be reseated in the last row of the orchestra section. I told them I would do my best to move some other ticket holders, and they insisted that I do so. I went to the back row and asked two very nice ladies if they would be willing to exchange seats. They looked at me with odd smiles and asked, "Does this have anything to do with Netanyahu?" Mind you, he had not entered the theater yet, and certainly there had been no public announcement of his being in attendance. My surprise must have been more obvious than I intended, and they quickly introduced themselves as off-duty FBI agents. Somehow, I actually felt more secure.

That didn't last long, though. With his back-row seats secured, Netanyahu quietly entered and took his seat—and immediately realized that seated directly next to him was the trade minister of Syria, a nation hostile to Israel.

Luckily, the overture began, and there was a peaceful international accord—at least during the performance of *The Lion King*.

Marc Forné Molné
Former Prime Minister of Andorra

When I was first told that the prime minister of Andorra was coming, I thought it sounded like a *Star Trek* planet—I had to go look it up and get versed in the fundamentals of its history and culture. I found that Andorra has an area of about 180 square miles and a population of eighty thousand. It has an annual armaments and defense budget of about a hundred dollars, for an honor guard to shoot rifle salutes for state events and celebrations. The prime minister later told me that it was easier to get into the United Nations than to get tickets to *The Lion King*. I was flattered that he loved the New Amsterdam. He also remarked, "Your usher staff outnumbers my army." Ultimately, and oddly, I was later made a knight of Andorra!

The exquisite interior of the New Amsterdam Theatre, New York City.

Pride Rock for Cubs

The Lion King Experience!

"When I was a kid, like in 1972, I remember distinctly subscribing to *Theatre Crafts* magazine and *The New Yorker*," recalls Thomas Schumacher, Disney Theatrical's president and producer. "Of course there was no Internet in those days. There was a library that had some books on theater, but those magazines were the only place I knew I could learn about current New York productions."

That spirit of curiosity and exploration has carried on through Schumacher's career, and he examines and

 I've seen nonverbal children find their voices in this show. I've seen students turn their lives around because they've realized their own potential. I've seen teachers discover their own artistry and infuse creativity into their classrooms. *The Lion King* is so much more than a musical. It heals. It inspires. It reminds us what it means to be alive.

 Lisa Mitchell, *Senior Manager, Education & Outreach,*
Disney Theatrical Productions

pursues every opportunity to connect theater with learning and to introduce students to the creativity and joy of the arts. To that end, the Disney Theatrical Productions team has created *The Lion King Experience!* It's an innovative and rigorous theater curriculum that helps schools and community groups bolster their arts-education offerings.

The Lion King is a show that offers—from its global inspirations and magnificent score to its design possibilities—a unique opportunity to create a sophisticated piece of art *with* young people. *The Lion King Experience!* includes a license to produce *The Lion King KIDS* or *The Lion King JR.*, shortened versions of the show that are appropriate for young performers. *The Lion King KIDS* is a thirty-minute, one-act rendition of the musical for elementary school students; *The Lion King JR.* is a seventy-minute, two-act version geared to middle school adolescents.

To date, some ten thousand student productions have been staged in auditoriums, gyms, and cafeterias across the United States and Canada, as well as in Great Britain and Australia. Disney estimates that some 250,000 young people have performed in one of the abridged versions of the show. Based on audience estimates of two hundred per show, that's an audience of 2.5 million very proud family members.

Open Doors

The Lion King *Goes to School*

The Open Doors education program, a collaboration of the Theatre Development Fund (TDF) with a variety of producers and shows including Disney Theatrical and *The Lion King*, provides mentors from the industry to work with high school students for the academic year and introduce them to theater.

In 1998, playwright Wendy Wasserstein and Broadway production stage manager Roy Harris joined with TDF to found the program in New York City. As Wasserstein put it, "Theater is a very personal experience that grows in meaning and depth when shared with others."

The Open Doors program pairs twenty-four selected New York City schools with distinguished theater and dance professionals who each mentor a group of eight students per school. Throughout the academic year, the students attend six live performances; each program is followed by a ninety-minute informal discussion between the students and their mentors. The students also keep journals to reflect on and document their experiences. At the end of the year, Open Doors celebrates with a ceremony to honor all the participants.

"I started going to the theater as a junior high school student, and I would go with a large group and get loaded into a theater in San Francisco, and it changed my life," Disney's Tom Schumacher says. "But if I could have gone to the theater with someone who *made* theater, I think my head would have exploded." It's the intimate connection—the feeling of impact—that inspires Schumacher, who has himself served as a mentor for over ten years. "They use this experience of going to the theater and talking about it with others to reveal things about themselves," he adds.

In 2011, Open Doors became the first arts education program to receive a special Tony Honor for Excellence in Theatre.

Thoughts and Feelings About *The Lion King* on Broadway

From some of the people who made it and make it run:

No matter who you are or where you are, the story of *The Lion King* speaks to you. The show crosses the great divides of race, class, and culture and is a story that everyone can relate to and understand. Every single person involved with the show brings this special piece of theater to life. Whether I'm onstage playing the Cheetah or off-stage laughing hysterically with friends, I feel alive when I'm at *The Lion King*, and for that I am forever grateful.

—**Lisa-Marie Lewis**, *Ensemble, Broadway company*

I first saw *The Lion King* at a press performance a few days before it opened. I went with my girlfriend (now my wife) and another couple. "Circle of Life" and the Procession were the most beautiful things I had ever seen in a theater. At the end of "Circle of Life," when I looked down my row at the three other fully grown people I had come with, they were all clapping, yelling with joy, and crying. I was crying, too—and I pretty much cry every time I see the opening of the show. It's hard to understand what the show did to the craft of theater when it opened, especially twenty years later, but *The Lion King* was revolutionary. The American theater had never seen anything like it.

—**Mimi Intagliata**, *Director, Production, Disney Theatrical Productions*

For many years, I was the company manager of the Broadway production, and when people asked me what the best thing was about my job, I always said that it is extremely satisfying and humbling to stand in the back of the house at the start of the show, and when the curtain rises and the giraffes start walking across the stage—and this beautiful show starts touching the audience—to be pretty much the only person who knows and works with every single person in that theater, from the box office crew and front-of-house staff to everyone backstage, from the child wrangler to the actor playing Mufasa climbing Pride Rock. That feeling always made me extremely proud.

—**Thomas Schlenk**, *General Manager, Broadway company*

I had never dreamed of playing the same character for such a long time—4,308 performances over thirteen years—but the impact that King Mufasa had on the child in all of us—and especially children of color—was something that I took very seriously. The responsibility of it continuously encouraged and inspired me to do my very best to honor being cast in the role of this iconic father figure, a gift with which Disney—and the universe—so faithfully entrusted me.

—**Alton Fitzgerald White**, *Mufasa, Broadway, Las Vegas, and Gazelle Tour companies*

I was *The Lion King* intern during the summer of 2001. It was a magical time for me. I worked with the project supervisor, producers, casting associate, and members of the creative team. One of the projects that I got to help with was *The Lion King* master classes, which were held for potential cast members. Sixteen years later, I work full time at Disney Theatrical.

—**Lisa Weiner,** *International Production Assistant, Disney Theatrcal Productions*

S inking into a reflective state, I was suddenly overcome by a wave of emotion during "He Lives in You," hearing Mufasa's disembodied voice, as if he was speaking directly to me. "You are more than what you have become. Remember who you are." I became completely unglued, as silent tears flowed down my face, my past, present, and future all intermingling in a moment of awakening. And that is why I love the theater. It has the power to inspire and awaken parts of ourselves we didn't

even realize were asleep. The experience of witnessing someone else's story provides a mirror into our own lives and informs our way of being in the world.

—**Michele Steckler,** *Assistant Director, original Broadway company, and Associate Producer, SVP Senior Producer, Disney Theatrical Productions*

O n the sixth floor of the New Amsterdam offices, there's a storage room chockablock full of metal flat files containing archived drawings and model pieces from every Disney show. In *The Lion King* area, there is a flat file drawer labeled SUPERSEDED, which has in it fully realized designs, hand-drawn on vellum, for a number of scenic pieces that never materialized in any production—Broadway or subsequently. For me, this flat file drawer is a monument to Julie Taymor's tenacity, never surrendering an idea. I can recall a number of times during the design process that Richard Hudson and our team were required by Julie to continue pursuing an idea—even when

For its first eight years on Broadway, The Lion King *lit up the marquee of the New Amsterdam Theatre.*

149

practical experience told us said idea was too complicated technically, or simply unaffordable. We later understood that a strong part of Julie's creative process involves an organic pursuit of ideas, which may evolve into other, perhaps realizable, better ideas.

—**Peter Eastman**, *Associate Set Designer, Broadway company*

In my position as production makeup supervisor, I have the privilege of watching the show every three weeks in order to maintain the integrity of the makeup designs. As I sit out there among the excited theatergoers—many of whom have never been to a Broadway show before—it is not lost on me how fortunate I am. Since I first discovered theater, there is no place I would rather be. I continue to be challenged and inspired by Michael Ward's beautiful makeup designs, which have evolved over the years. To me *The Lion King* is a living, breathing thing, and knowing how much it has touched so many people has been the gratifying icing on the cake.

—**Elizabeth Cohen**, *Makeup Department Head, Broadway company*

The Lion King company is truly a family for the kids in the cast. We are with them more than they are their actual families during their time with the show. All the Young Simbas and Nalas learn from the people around them. We are a huge part of their childhood. And we have helped to raise some awesome kids! I will never forget how the entire company came together to rally around

Shannon [Tavarez, who played Young Nala] during her leukemia treatments. Shannon was my girl, and every Monday I would gather that week's massive number of gifts from the cast and company and make the trip out to Queens to be the bearer of good tidings and well-wishes. Every week there was a new wig from Jon Jordan, our head of hair, art projects from the ushers, games from the musicians. *The Lion King* is a family, and we take care of our own.

—**Niki White**, *"Kid Wrangler," Broadway company*

The hardest thing for me was performing the day after the World Trade Center went down on 9/11. So much about the attack was unknown, and it was difficult and scary to do the show. So many people lost their lives that day, but when the curtain went up the very next day, it was up to us to uplift the audience and to make them, and ourselves, feel that everything would be all right. We had to move on and not let the terrorists win.

—**Lindiwe Dlamini**, *Ensemble, Broadway company*

Anytime I need a boost in my spirits, I watch the opening number, "Circle of Life," and the audience reaction always alters my emotional state in an extremely positive way."

—**Pam Young**, *Director, Creative Development, Disney Theatrical Productions*

Oops! Live on Broadway

"Everybody who works on Broadway has tales of stage horrors," says Tom Schumacher, "and we've had some doozies on *The Lion King*. Among the craziest was the night that Simba had gotten very, very sick and couldn't go on. So, the understudy, who was well rehearsed and ready to perform, suddenly comes down with the flu—*bad* flu. There was no way he could go on. The third guy—there are always three—*could* go on, but he had never performed in front of an audience, and he wasn't fully rehearsed, so we were getting him up to speed as the house was about to open. The last thing he had to practice was swinging onto the stage on a vine for the 'Hakuna Matata' number at the end of the first act. So out he swings, and he lands wrong, spraining his ankle. There wasn't a single person in the theater who could play Simba.

"*But* production stage manager Jeff Lee did some fast thinking. He remembered we had a former Simba understudy five blocks up the street," adds Schumacher, "performing in our production of *Aida* at the Palace Theatre, a lovely guy named Tim Hunter, who was one of the original giraffes. So, we called stage management and they threw a robe on him and walked him down here after arranging for his *Aida* swing to go on in his place. Now he hadn't played Simba for two years, so while the audience was watching act one, Tim was getting made up and put into his costume and running his lines.

"And when Adult Simba swung onto stage at the end of 'Hakuna Matata' that night," notes Schumacher, "no one in the audience had the slightest idea what had gone on. And *that's* Broadway!"

Back when the very tall, slender Kissy Vaughan was playing Nala, she fell ill after singing "Shadowland" and couldn't continue the show. The only Nala cover in the building was the very pregnant Rema Webb. She was thrown into makeup and costume and was ready just in time to enter and say the line "There's no food . . . no water. . . ." It was a kind of hilarious visual incongruence. Nala's belly had grown exponentially since her last scene!

 Elizabeth Cohen, *Production Makeup Supervisor, Broadway company*

The North American Tours

***If the People Can't Come to* The Lion King,
Then The Lion King *Will Go to the People!***

The Lion King has been touring North America now for fifteen years—
with no plans to stop.

The Gazelle Tour

This, the first *Lion King* tour, opened on April 27, 2002, at the Buell
Theatre in Denver, and closed on July 23, 2017, in Houston at the
Hobby Center. It played 6,247 performances, which is 110 more than the
entire original run of *A Chorus Line*, the sixth longest running show in
Broadway history.

The Cheetah Tour

One tour couldn't meet the country's demand for seats, so a second
North American tour was launched. It opened May 3, 2003, at the
Cadillac Palace Theatre in Chicago, and closed on March 2, 2008, at the
Milwaukee Theatre in Wisconsin's largest city. Over 4.5 million people
saw its 1,927 performances.

The Rafiki Tour

In October 2017, a third North American tour hit the road, making its
debut at the Landmark Theatre in Syracuse, New York. The newly con-
figured production will allow the musical to play in cities and venues that
could not previously accommodate it. This state-of-the-art production,
which uses technology that wasn't available when the first tour launched
in 2002, will be more nimble and adaptable than the Gazelle Tour, but
equal in size, scale, scope, and spectacle.

Gerald Ramsey as Mufasa in the first North American tour.

Mukelisiwe Goba as Rafiki and Aaron Nelson as Simba.

Patrick R. Brown (left) and Gerald Ramsey.

I had been the associate conductor with the Gazelle Tour for just over a year when I experienced the single most meaningful day in my career in theater—the first sensory-friendly performance on tour, in July 2011 in Houston. As I was not conducting, I spent most of the show wandering around the house in tears at the way the entire theater pulsed with abject joy and wonder, expressed in every imaginable way. I was lost in my own emotional mix of awe and sadness and joy, spiced with deep empathy. Three years later, I conducted the sensory-friendly show in Boston, and eight months after that, my own beautiful daughter, Remi, was born with Down syndrome. *The Lion King* has given me many gifts, in addition to the obvious ones: I met my wife, Nina, on the road; we have had two children, Ethan and Remi, on the road; our family knows only life as blissful wanderers, a strange and fantastic way to form family bonds. And not only our nuclear family, but the greater family that is the Gazelle Tour.

Conducting the show nightly, I have the best seat in the house to see the show, and also to see and feel the families around me, sharing moments of awe, heartbreak, and love. Art. Life. Touring has broadened my perspective on theater, on art, on what it means to be a friend, a colleague, a music director, a parent. I am so grateful to work for a company that actively supports Remi and my family, as well as communities with special needs everywhere we travel.

 Jamie Schmidt, *Music Director, Gazelle Tour*

In the beautiful Majestic Theatre in San Antonio, there was a bat that lived in the theater. Apparently, the bat wasn't getting enough excitement scaring people backstage, so one night it flew out onto the stage during the Grasslands scene! It circled Pride Rock a few times, and then when Zazu entered, it began to circle Zazu while he sang "The Morning Report," and then flew out over the audience's heads several times! After the song ended, the show was stopped (which was just as well, since the audience was spending much more of their attention on the bat than the show). The bat was captured, gently, and set free outdoors, and the performance resumed.

 Tony Freeman, *Zazu, Gazelle Tour*

Drew Hirschfield.

 In April of 2012, *The Lion King* became the first Broadway show to have one million "likes" on Facebook. The number is now more than 2.5 million.

I remember one night, many years ago, when we were opening in Michigan. I thought the venue had a terrible sound, and it was hard to get the show right in there. At the end of one performance, the audience was leaving, and I was frustrated and angry because it hadn't sounded good to me, and I felt like every choice I made was wrong, and that I had ruined the show. A huge man approached me as I was shutting the console down; he was dressed like he'd come in from the fields, and had a huge beard—definitely not a "theater guy." He came up to me, and I thought he was going to complain. Instead, he said quietly, "Thank you, thank you," and began to choke up with tears. "'They Live in You' . . . I had no idea it could be like that. Amazing. . . ." As he walked away, I was so moved, I don't even remember if I said anything.

🦌 **Kevin Higley,** *Sound Department, Gazelle Tour*

Aaron Nelson.

The evening of the very first out-of-town preview of *The Lion King* was the beginning of an incredible journey for everyone involved in the show. I am still the "guy in the field" for Disney Theatrical and am so happy to have brought *The Lion King* to audiences throughout North America—from Anchorage to Miami and everywhere in between. Every first performance in a city brings the same excitement that we experienced in Minneapolis in 1997, and audiences still respond just as enthusiastically every night. I'm honored to have worked on two hundred engagements and eight thousand performances . . . and counting. Thank you, Minneapolis, and all the millions of theater-lovers who have embraced *The Lion King* since 1997.

🦌 **Jack Eldon,** *Vice President Domestic Touring, Disney Theatrical Productions*

Other American Productions

The first American production outside New York premiered in Los Angeles on October 19, 2000, at the freshly renovated Pantages Theatre, which was originally built in 1930. That's just down Hollywood Boulevard from the El Capitan, the Disney-owned movie theater where *The Lion King* film had its initial run. Coincidentally, the Pantages, at Vine Street, is just across the intersection from the old Broadway department store, where one of *Lion King* producer Tom Schumacher's early jobs was selling ladies' shoes. And composer Lebo M. once had a job parking cars at a lot across the street from the theater. The Los Angeles production closed in January 2003; its set was then used for the Cheetah Tour.

A third American production of *The Lion King* opened a few years later at the Mandalay Bay Resort and Casino in Las Vegas on April 20, 2009. It was the first Disney Theatrical production ever to open there. While Broadway musicals had set down on the Strip before, nearly all of them had severely cut their shows to fit a ninety-minute format. Schumacher and Disney Theatrical, however, resisted, presenting the whole show to visitors entering the "Entertainment Capital of the World." *The Lion King* ran in Las Vegas until New Year's Eve, 2011.

I had the privilege of playing Nala for nine consecutive years—making history as the longest-running actor in that role. I originated the tour and stayed with it for a year. Then I moved to Broadway for six years, after which I opened with the Las Vegas company, where I played for two years. The last matinee of my run was when the walls came tumbling down. As I broke from the pack to sing "Shadowland," I could not get past the first lyric. Nine years flashed before me, and a lump the size of Africa formed in my throat. Strong, fierce Nala the lion became a weak kitten. The conductor gave the cue for the orchestra to play as softly as they possibly could, and I stood onstage with tears rolling down my face, barely singing. A momentous chapter of my life had come to an end, and the unknown was about to begin. But this I knew—my Pride will always be with me. Family.

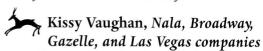 **Kissy Vaughan,** *Nala, Broadway, Gazelle, and Las Vegas companies*

Kissy Vaughan.

I started working as Disney's theatrical consultant prior to the opening of *Beauty and the Beast*, an unexpected hit that convinced Disney that Broadway and subsequent tours could be incredibly lucrative. The theater division was quickly restructured to be run by animation executives Peter Schneider and Thomas Schumacher.

With new leadership in charge, my assignment was up for review. I remember sitting outside Tom's office in Burbank, having no idea what would happen. But I was excited by the prospect of working with two men who were both smart and well respected—and who came from theater. Two minutes into the meeting we were mapping out strategy to announce Disney's next Broadway offering: *The Lion King*, directed by Julie Taymor.

Patrick R. Brown as Scar and Gerald Ramsey as Mufasa on tour.

There were all kinds of questions. How were we going to sell a musical about animals played by people? Could *The Lion King* match the success of *Beauty*? Would the new leadership be able to handle two shows on Broadway? Would *The Lion King* even work onstage? Julie was confident, but I was fretful—needlessly as it turned out, of course.

I was one of the team that moved to Minneapolis for the run of the out-of-town tryout. Word had gotten out that Julie had beautifully and uniquely reimagined the highly beloved film, and journalists began making the trip to Minnesota. Press features were lining up rapidly, and our Broadway campaign was off and running. By the time we left Minneapolis, we had sold $40 million in tickets for the Broadway run.

That whole year may have been the most exhilarating of my career. Every single day brought some new challenge, new triumph, or fantastic piece of news. I was working alongside the great Nancy Coyne and Rick Elice of the Serino Coyne advertising agency, and we would all run over to the Disney offices to have daily meetings with Peter and Tom. We would discuss the day's challenges and triumphs, plan and laugh, and decide which news outlets we would let tell our story—a luxury that rarely happens in this business!

Talk about heady days! It's an unbelievable charge when a show you care about becomes an instant smash hit.

All of us thought *The Lion King* deserved all the Tonys it would eventually win, but we also wanted the Broadway community to know that Disney was all in for the long haul. When Nathan Lane opened the envelope at the Tony Awards and announced that *The Lion King* was the year's Best Musical, the Tony voters didn't just honor an important new musical, they opened a new door to Disney on Broadway. Nothing would ever be quite the same.

—Chris Boneau, *Partner/Co-Owner, Boneau/Bryan-Brown Theatrical Public Relations*

Is that . . . *Whoopi Goldberg*?!?

They didn't know it when the houselights went down for the beginning of the show, but the audience at the evening performance of *The Lion King* on Wednesday, February 3, 2010, were in for a particularly special treat—and one that none of the ticket holders could possibly have anticipated.

The show began with its cry in the dark, the evocative South African chanting of the chorus, and the voice of

Rafiki singing "Circle of Life." The shimmering silk sun rose from the stage floor and a procession of enchantingly creative African animals began to descend through the orchestra of the Minskoff Theatre.

That's when people started to notice. That actress in the white costume, with the bird on her head? Holding up another bird in each hand . . . ? Is that possibly Whoopi Goldberg? It *looks* like Whoopi Goldberg. It *is* Whoopi

Producer Thomas Schumacher and director Julie Taymor greet Whoopi Goldberg backstage at the Minskoff Theatre.

Whoopi Goldberg, the film's voice of Shenzi, became a Disney Legend in July 2017.

Shenzi in the 1994 *Lion King* film. "But that was *hard*, those things they have to walk around on. There's a certain coordination of moving your costume leg without looking at your real leg. It's a whole thing. So I kind of did my own version of a hyena.

"It's all much harder than you think," she contends. "Even the graceful bird lady is hard, because you're holding your arms straight out. And there's no lowering the birds. The birds stay up, and you're making them flap while you walk."

What is it about the show that's so special to Goldberg? "I love this show. That opening scene is one of the most extraordinary things ever produced for a Broadway stage. I love it more than anyone could imagine, because it gets kids excited when they see it. They think, 'Oh, I would like to do that,' and that's something I want to be part of, something that excites a kid and makes them want to try something new."

Goldberg! By the time she stepped onto the stage, everyone in the theater knew the comic/actress/talk show icon was in the house—actually not just "in the house," but "in the show!"

"It was something we cooked up for *The View*," remembers Goldberg, one of only five actors ever to win an Oscar, Emmy, Tony, *and* Grammy. And ABC-TV's *The View*, which Whoopi joined in 2007, got it all on tape, airing a segment tracing Goldberg's one-off gig, rehearsing during the day and performing that night. (You can find the segment on YouTube.)

But the audience was going to see Whoopi more than once. She'd soon be back, done up in the elaborate mandrill-inspired makeup and costume of the shamanic Rafiki. The actress, who has appeared numerous times on Broadway, swung in on a rope, reprising a sight gag she once offered up at the Tony Awards.

"I really wanted to try the hyenas, fool that I am," says Goldberg, who famously provided the voice for

A puzzled Rafiki (Tshidi Manye) and Simba (DaShaun Young) meet another Rafiki (Whoopi Goldberg).

When The *Lion King* opened on Broadway in the fall of 1997, I was braying out "Hakuna Matata" as Pumbaa, the flatulent warthog. Thirteen years passed—the new millennium arrived. America went to war. They invented the iPod. Still I was a warthog.

Did playing the same role over 5,500 times drive me mad? This assumes I was sane to begin with, which is rarely the case with actors. (What reasonable person would wade through years of rejection on the off chance that someday he will be allowed to smear makeup on his face, glue a ratty wig on his head, and declaim, "The Queen, my lord, is dead"?)

During my years in *Lion King*, the physical therapist became my best friend. Two knee operations and one shoulder surgery; my spinal disks melted like the snows of Kilimanjaro. Still, I strapped on my fifty-pound puppet and leaped into the jungle with the friskiness of a spring lamb. Is there any other profession where the show must go on so desperately? Must the transmission be repaired? Must the spreadsheet be spread?

You would think, given the difficulty of supporting oneself in the theater, that staying in a long run would be considered a good thing. This illusion was shattered by the director, Julie Taymor herself, who greeted me after year two of my "stint" by asking kindly, "Are you *looking* for other work?" In fact, Disney was generous enough to let me take short leaves to perform in another Broadway show titled *Is He Dead?*, *Henry V* in New York's Central Park, two Encores! shows, and numerous workshops and readings. But I always returned to the warmth and security of my purple puppet.

I believe there are things you can learn about the craft of acting in a long run that you can't learn anywhere else. Tension is the enemy of creativity, and I defy you to remain tense when you're doing performance number five thousand and ten—you're more likely to be as loose as overcooked spaghetti. A long run also affords the time to develop an incredibly rich inner monologue. For the benefit of future theater historians, I have re-created a tiny bit of my inner monologue during the "Hakuna Matata" scene that ends act 1:

Oh, God, my back hurts. Better hop around . . . get the blood moving. Don't want to hyperventilate again when I scream at the buzzards. Boy, this audience is quiet. OK, here we go. Oy, I'm stuffed. I can't eat paella before a show. I'm so stupid. Aaand . . . [I leap out onstage to begin the scene.] Don't land on the bad knee. Who's that playing the buzzard? Is he new? I've got to start reading the call-board. OK, see the

Tom Alan Robbins.

baby lion. Did he move? Whoa, I think it's still alive. Better tell Timon. Wait, I got a note on this. What was it? Open the mouth wider? Be more terrified? Shoot! I'll get it next time. Crap, it's my line! Wider, wider, let 'em see the tonsils. I hope someone from management is watching. Don't get distracted. Listen, listen. That's right; it means "no worries." Pick up the tempo. Sell it! Sell it!

And this is how it went, eight times a week, twelve months a year, for thirteen years. My parting was a simple one—a cake and a human sacrifice, and the pig was passed to its new owner, Ben Jeffrey. Seven years later, I have finally stopped singing "Hakuna Matata" in my sleep, much to my wife's relief. There is life after *Lion King*, and it is much, much easier on the back.

—Tom Alan Robbins, *Pumbaa, original Broadway company*

 *Movin' On Up—Three Blocks North*

Moving *The Lion King* from the New Amsterdam to the Minskoff Theatre in 2006 was a risky decision. The New Am had been home for many years, and the show was running like clockwork—the cast, crew, and audiences were happy. But for a whole host of reasons—mainly to make the New Am available for *Mary Poppins,* which was coming in from London—we made the decision to march the show up the street. One of my primary responsibilities during the move was overseeing the design and installation of the yellow-and-black *Lion King* logo in the lobby windows, a sign that has now become iconic. It's huge—two stories tall and nearly a New York City block wide.

The moment that sign lit up, glowing like a beacon into the heart of Times Square, I knew we'd found our second home. It was magnificent! People stopped to take photos with the sign as their backdrop. Since then, every New Year's Eve, I watch Times Square from home on the television, and I see that sign in the background, always there, always standing proud, always beckoning people to see our wonderful show, and I'm filled with joy thinking about the millions of people whose hearts have been forever changed by the beauty of our work.

—Andrew Flatt, *SVP, Strategy, Marketing & Revenue, Disney Theatrical Productions*

The Lion King and the Autism Theatre Initiative

On October 2, 2011, *The Lion King* played host to the Autism Theatre Initiative's first-ever autism-friendly performance of a Broadway show. A project of the Theatre Development Fund (TDF), which is dedicated to making theater accessible to all audiences, the Autism Theatre Initiative is designed to create a safe environment for children and adults on the autism spectrum and their families. Parents of children with autism typically avoid entertainment situations because of sensory intensity and surprise, and because those on the spectrum can sometimes have tics that cause them to make loud noises; or they need to get up and move around.

Everything about the theater, from the lobby to the auditorium, is rethought for the safety and comfort of this unique audience. The stage performance itself includes reductions of sound volume, softening or removal of strobes and other lighting or audio elements, and "blue-outs" rather than blackouts.

Recently, I volunteered for the third time at *The Lion King*'s autism-friendly performance. This time, though, I was at the front of the house facing the audience. The show started, and as the animals started coming down the aisle, I was able to see all these kids' and their families' reactions, and I totally broke down. I could not stop crying. I don't know if I have ever felt so satisfied and happy in my life. I could not be prouder of where I work. The realization that this show could affect so many people and be something special to so many was overwhelming, and is overwhelming, in all the best ways.

 Noel Moore, *Senior Business Analyst, Disney Theatrical Productions*

ABOVE AND LEFT: *Volunteers and guests at the Minskoff Theatre for the Autism Theatre Initiative.*

On October 20, 2013, *The Lion King* became the first Broadway show ever to earn more than one *billion* dollars.

W hen we started doing performances for the special-needs kids and their families, it changed me, and made me appreciate what I do onstage even more. It is very hard for these families to go to a regular Broadway show as a family. We have people all over the building to make sure their needs are taken care of in order for them to enjoy the show with no pressure or worry. It's the most amazing thing to witness.

 Lindiwe Dlamini, *Ensemble, Broadway company*

"Every minute of our special [autism performances] is spectacular," Thomas Schumacher told *Playbill*. "Families come, and the experience they're having is one that they can't really have any other time, where they can be totally free and just let go and enjoy the evening."

Since the first of many *Lion King* autism-friendly performances, other musicals—and even nonmusicals—have enthusiastically come on board and joined the program. Disney shows in the program have included both *Mary Poppins* and *Aladdin*. Carrying the message to a younger demographic, the Autism Theatre Initiative partnered again with Disney with the first-ever autism-friendly performance of *Disney Junior Live on Tour: Pirate and Princess Adventure* at The Theater at Madison Square Garden.

And the program has expanded beyond Broadway to productions in Boston, Houston, Pittsburgh, and Minneapolis.

The Lion King—*Popping Up All Over*

In 2012, to celebrate fifteen years on Broadway, Disney Theatrical mounted a free, interactive exhibition of eighty-six set drawings, models, masks, costumes, and other artifacts from the show. Called "Inside *The Lion King*," the five-thousand-square-foot "pop-up gallery" opened on December 1 at the corner of Forty-Second Street and Avenue of the Americas, opposite Bryant Park. The "now you see it/now you don't" run, which featured "guest appearances" by Madame Tussauds's wax renditions of Rafiki and Scar, lasted only sixteen days.

Rafiki at Madame Tussauds.

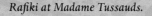

劇団四季
www.shiki.gr.jp
©Disney
王の血が騒ぎ出す。
生命の連鎖の神秘を
壮大なスケールで描いて
未到のロングランはつづく。
Disney's
ライオンキング
新名古屋ミュージカル劇場
主催：劇団四季／中日新聞社／東海テレビ放送
協賛：積水ハウス／明治乳業　協力：JR東海

PART III

THE ROAR HEARD ROUND THE WORLD

In 2017, Disney Theatrical Productions is one of the world's most successful producers of musicals in the international arena, where its shows compete with other instantly recognizable titles like *Wicked*, *Mamma Mia!*, and British uber-producer Cameron Mackintosh's crowd-pleasers—*Cats*, *The Phantom of the Opera*, and *Les Misérables* among them.

But Disney had to learn about the global theater market from the ground up, on the fly—and fast—much as they did the intricacies and potential pitfalls of producing on Broadway itself. "When we first produced *Beauty and Beast*," says Ron Kollen, senior vice president of international productions, who has been with Disney Theatrical for over twenty years, "I don't think anybody realized the global scope of doing a Broadway musical. But when

promoters in other countries began coming to us saying, 'You have this hit on Broadway and we want to do it in our country,' Michael Eisner began to understand that musicals had a life beyond Broadway and an American tour. After the success of our overseas productions of

OPPOSITE: *A poster from the first international production in Tokyo, Japan.*

RIGHT: *Loading in the set in Tokyo's Shiki Theatre Haru.*

The Circustheater in Scheveningen, Netherlands, has been home to two productions of The Lion King.

Beauty and the Beast, Eisner saw past the obvious benefit of revenue to the long-term value of getting the brand out there in an entirely new way, offering live entertainment in new markets."

Disney musicals are now staged abroad in one of two ways. In most of the English-speaking world (particularly the United Kingdom and Australia), Disney Theatrical itself produces the shows. In non-English markets, the company licenses the show to local partners. Productions may be "sit-down," which means self-contained and usually open-ended, or they may be part of a tour. Disney titles are so sought-after that some presenters are willing to renovate or even build a new theater to house them. Theaters in Seoul, Johannesburg, and Mexico City were purposely built to accommodate *The Lion King*.

Sets on the Move

At the moment, Disney juggles ten complete *Lion King* sets. Some are permanent fixtures of long-running productions, while others hop around the planet. The original Australian set went to Johannesburg, for example. The current Shanghai set will travel on the first international tour, which kicks off in Manila, Philippines, in 2018.

When one of the two North American tours ended, the remaining tour started using two leapfrogging sets, with one loaded into a new theater while the show was performed in another city. When not in use, the sets go into storage. They are also frequently spruced up and refitted, with the fabric legs and cloud borders tending to need replacing most often. "I always say that we haven't *lowered* the ticket price since opening night," remarks production supervisor Doc Zorthian, "so the set should always look as good as opening night—if not better."

With so many productions running around the world, we would often get about ten show reports in a day. Most of the time, they were pretty standard. Every once in a while, though, something out of the ordinary would come through.

Over the years, I collected reports that stood out or made me laugh: "Someone put their chewing gum on the grass during the show. An investigation will begin!" "No rhino for 'Circle of Life' (the artist wasn't aware of his part)." "Kind of acceptable show, not overwhelming. Anyway, immediate standing ovation."

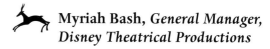 **Myriah Bash,** *General Manager, Disney Theatrical Productions*

The Lion King's first production in Spanish opened in Madrid in 2011.

The Lion King *International Productions*

TOKYO, Japan
Shiki Theatre Natsu
December 1998–present

OSAKA, Japan
Osaka Shiki Theatre
April 1999–January 2001
Japanese National Tour

LONDON, U.K.
Lyceum Theatre
October 1999–present

TORONTO, Canada
Princess of Wales Theatre
April 2000–January 2004

FUKUOKA, Japan
Fukuoka City Theatre
April 2001–March 2003
Japanese National Tour

HAMBURG, Germany
Stage Theater im Hafen
December 2001–present

NAGOYA, Japan
Shin Nagoya Musical
Theatre
June 2003–January 2006
Japanese National Tour

SYDNEY, Australia
Capitol Theatre
October 2003–June 2005
Australian National Tour

SCHEVENINGEN,
Netherlands
Circustheater
April 2004–August 2006

MELBOURNE, Australia
Regent Theatre
July 2005–June 2006
Australian National Tour

SHANGHAI, China
Shanghai Grand Theatre
July 2006–October 2006
Australian National Tour

SEOUL, South Korea
Charlotte Theater
October 2006–October
2007

JOHANNESBURG,
South Africa
Teatro at Montecasino
May 2007–February 2008

PARIS, France
Théâtre Mogador
October 2007–July 2010

FUKUOKA, Japan (2)
Fukuoka City Theatre
January 2008–August 2009
Japanese National Tour

TAIPEI, Taiwan
Taipei Dome
August 2008
Australian National Tour

SAPPORO, Japan
Hokkaido Shiki Theatre
March 2011–September
2012
Japanese National Tour

SINGAPORE
Marina Bay Sands Theatre
March 2011–October 2011

MADRID, Spain
Teatro Lope de Vega
October 2011–present

UNITED KINGDOM
TOUR
September 2012–October
2015
Nine cities in England,
plus Scotland
(Edinburgh), Wales
(Cardiff), and the
Republic of Ireland
(Dublin)

OSAKA, Japan (2)
Osaka Shiki Theatre
October 2012–May 2016

SÃO PAULO, Brazil
Teatro Renault
March 2013–December
2014

AUSTRALIA TOUR (2)
December 2013–February
2016
Sydney, Melbourne,
Brisbane, and Perth

BASEL, Switzerland
Musical Theater Basel
March 2015–October 2015
United Kingdom Tour

MEXICO CITY, Mexico
Teatro Telcel
May 2015–present

SHANGHAI, China
Shanghai Disney Resort
June 2016–October 2017

SCHEVENINGEN,
Netherlands (2)
Circustheater
October 2016–present

SAPPORO, Japan (2)
Hokkaido Shiki Theatre
March 2017–present

First INTERNATIONAL
TOUR
March 2018
The tour kicks off in
Manila, the capital of
the Philippines, and will
play in multiple cities
throughout Southeast
Asia and the world.

Also coming in 2018:
An all-new tour sets out
in the United Kingdom.

The Lion Tamers: Maintaining the Pride

In the jungle, the lion may sleep at night, but *The Lion King* never rests—at least it's never out of production. That's why Disney Theatrical employs a staff of twenty-one theater artists, technicians, and managers who create and keep watch over all the companies worldwide. They're responsible for everything onstage at all new and continuing manifestations of the show.

This core group reports to Anne Quart, senior vice president of production and coproducer of Disney Theatrical Productions, who has been with the company for fifteen years. Each one of these worldwide productions—currently there are ten—also has a *resident* creative staff (director, choreographer, etc.) that works with the visiting core team and maintains the musical when they depart.

Overall, Quart estimates there are some two thousand people employed by *The Lion King* globally, including vendors who take care of building sets, making puppets, and producing costumes.

One of the most challenging aspects of coordinating the core team is scheduling. "It's a massive undertaking to figure out the matrix of where everybody is," says Quart, "because there's no point in having the music department do a cleanup with the company in Hamburg, for example, if we can't also get the sound department there at the same time.

"For instance, when we were starting to tech our new North American tour in Syracuse in upstate New York," Quart recounts, "the only puppet person we could schedule to get the show on its feet was the guy from Germany. It's all incredibly international. The Africa/Asia tour will have a South African musical director, a Mexican resident director, and the resident dance supervisor from Shanghai."

Quart actually understates the predicament creative teams face when she notes that it's "tricky" to make sure all the necessary people are in the right places all the time. "We sit down and just go through the calendar and figure it out," Quart notes. "Say we know we're opening a new production in Scheveningen in the Netherlands, but we're also doing auditions for Rafiki in South Africa, and we want to do cleanups in London and Madrid, plus Germany is having a cast change. So one group of our guys will go to Scheveningen to put the new production together with our producing partner over there, and another group will go to Germany, South Africa, London, and Madrid to take care of the cleanup stuff, which we do for every production about twice a year.

"During the few times when we have no new show being mounted and we have one of the directing associates available," Quart continues, "we take a look at the worldwide situation to see what company would benefit from a more protracted work period. John Stefaniuk, for example, had six weeks in the early part of the spring, so we decided to plant him New York and have him spend some real time with the Broadway company. Last year we did it with London."

The "cleanups" are not, in fact, because anyone is doing anything wrong. It's just a way of keeping *The Lion King* production as crisp and clean years into its run as it was on opening night. "Of course everyone in the principal cast suffers from a performance that has strayed from the original intent," says Quart, "but the ensemble is the most vulnerable. It's easy for the ensemble to go out and hit the blocking, be in the elephant, be in the gazelle, but they can forget about the story they're meant to be telling. Julie Taymor still does cleanup when we can make the schedule work. This is the time to remind people who are new to the show about the motivation behind each gesture, the reason for every move.

"Even three hours with Julie can recharge a company for six months," Quart contends. "Lebo has the same effect. Michael Curry just went through every single puppet and headdress with the Broadway puppet department to make sure every detail is right."

When all is said and done, the function of this frequent-flying staff is to keep Julie Taymor's vision alive and well around the planet. "I talk to her frequently," says Quart, "and I feel strongly about remaining connected to her. *The Lion King* is so big now and it's been going on for so long that it's easy to take for granted. My mantra for years has been, 'The minute you take *The Lion King* for granted, it starts to erode.'

"And being connected to Julie helps me avoid that," Quart adds. "She worked with the New York cast recently on some changes we wanted to make for the show's twentieth anniversary, and I have to say I just love watching her work.

"Those of us who have worked on *The Lion King* and continue to work on *The Lion King* are always aware that this is a once-in-a-lifetime experience. Part of what makes it unique is the global scope and longevity of the show," Quart says. "But more than that, everybody still loves each other. And that is rare in any twenty-year endeavor. *The Lion King* is a family, for sure."

The Core Staff for The Lion King Worldwide

As of August 2017

Production Supervisor Doc Zorthian
General Manager Thomas Schlenk
Associate General Manager Michael Height
Associate Director John Stefaniuk
Associate Choreographer Marey Griffith
Music Supervisor Clement Ishmael
Dance Supervisor Celise Hicks
Supervising Resident Director Anthony Lyn
Associate Music Supervisor David Kreppel
Associate Scenic Designer Peter Eastman
Associate Costume Designer Mary Nemecek Peterson
Associate Mask & Puppet Designer Louis Troisi
Assistant Mask & Puppet Designer Mike Grimm
Associate Sound Designer John Shivers
Assistant Sound Designer Hugh Sweeney
Associate Hair & Makeup Designer Rowena Hume
Associate Lighting Designer Carolyn Wong
Lighting Supervisor Jeanne Koenig
Assistant Lighting Designer Marty Vreeland
Automated Lighting Designer Aland Henderson
Production Coordinator Christina Huschle

There are no Africans in the Japanese production, but their Rafiki is Ainu, the indigenous people of Hokkaido, who are much more aligned with the *sangoma*, the shamans from South Africa. And their Timon and Pumbaa spoke in an Okinawan accent, because apparently people in Tokyo think of people from Okinawa as country folk. Of course, the Japanese have a wonderful tradition of masks and puppetry, and so they excelled far beyond the Westerners in all that work.

Julie Taymor, *Director*

TOKYO, JAPAN

DECEMBER 1998–PRESENT

International interest in *The Lion King* began even before the show opened. Representatives of the Shiki Theatre Company, which had produced *Beauty and the Beast* in Japan, flew to Minneapolis to scout the out-of-town tryout. Not only were they certain that they wanted to produce it, they wanted to do it first (Austria and Australia had produced *Beauty* before them).

Shiki (Japanese for "four seasons") is one of the largest theater companies in the world. It was founded in 1953 by Keita Asari, an impresario whose decades of credits include the opening ceremonies of the 1998 Winter Olympics in Nagano. The company's eight hundred actors, technicians, and managers stage up to three thousand performances a year in the company's nine theaters. Shiki began training Japanese actors in the disciplines of Western musicals after a visiting production of *West Side Story* in 1964 and produced its own first musical, *Applause*, in 1972.

Since their original multiple productions of *Beauty and the Beast* and *The Lion King*, Shiki has also staged *Aida*, *The Little Mermaid*, *Aladdin*, and *The Hunchback of Notre Dame* (a Disney show that has actually never appeared on Broadway despite having success in Europe and Asia). *The Lion King* production in Tokyo opened on December 20, 1998, at the brand-new 1,255-seat Shiki Theatre Haru; it has been the longest continually running show in Japanese theater history, although it was recently moved to the Shiki Theatre Natsu to allow for the renovation of the Haru. A second Shiki production of *The Lion King* has been playing in Osaka, Fukuoka, Nagoya, and Sapporo on a rotating basis since April 1999.

Not the New Amsterdam Anymore

Jeff Lee, the original Broadway production stage manager, who later went on to a dozen international productions as associate director, had a rude awakening when the creative team first went to Tokyo to meet the Shiki Theater Company. After all, the show had only been done once at that point, and it was done the best way the Broadway cast and crew could do it. Tokyo was like a new world entirely.

The first non-English production was [in] Japan, and I couldn't sleep because I didn't know how I was going to teach African music to the Japanese cast. But after the first half hour, I noticed that Japanese vowels are much closer in sound and pronunciation to South African languages, and the performers there catch on faster than English speakers because they hear the vowel quicker. When I say "*busa le lizwe*" or whatever else has been very complicated for Americans or Brits, the Japanese pronounce it exactly right by the third try. I spent less time teaching the "*nants' ingonyama*" opening in Japan than any other country.

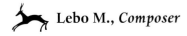 **Lebo M.,** *Composer*

LEFT: *Tomonari Shibuya as Scar woos
Mariko Machi as Nala in Tokyo.*

BELOW: *Shiki Theatre Company's
Akito Minami as Simba.*

For one thing, there would be no South Africans in the cast. Shiki supports hundreds of actors, and all the casting would be done from inside the company. And the parts would be cast with performers in constant rotation. The Broadway production uses about forty backstage crew, including dressers. Shiki offered five backstage managers. Period! The cast did its own makeup, helped each other with quick changes, and even washed and repaired their own costumes, wigs, and puppets. Lee was stunned.

"My first reaction was it just couldn't be done their way," he says. "They had to do it the way we had done it. But I just had to let that go. After all, they have been doing theater in Japan for a very long time, and this is how they do it. We

Every dancer, every actor is different, and it makes sense to use those differences, not to try to fit everyone into the same mold. Our first Simba in Japan was an Olympic gymnast, so I gave him things to do that no other Simba after him could ever do—putting in an extra tumble or two for his entrance, for example. So there are many subtle differences between *The Lion King* in Japan and in New York, just as there are between all the productions.

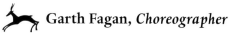 **Garth Fagan,** *Choreographer*

*T*here is no stage magic in *The Lion King*, but its power and charm are unquestionably magical. Perhaps that is why it brings a quiet, creative revolution to any country it visits, breaking down boundaries. How wondrous that is!

Koichi Tanaka, *Executive Director, Shiki Theatre Company*

had to let the company work their way. In the end, I just decided that if what hit the proscenium on opening night was what the Disney creative team wanted to see, then any road to getting there was as good as any other."

Having the Japanese experience also helped frame the staging of all future productions. "It really helped us to see that our job wasn't going in there and handing them our completed show beat by beat in every detail. We were there to work with them to discover the show on their own terms, to allow each company and each actor to breathe their own experiences, their own national characters, their own senses of humor into the template of Julie Taymor's *Lion King*.

"So as we started traveling around the world," Lee continues, "we weren't thinking that we are there to tame the locals into doing something set in stone. We wanted to give the companies and their audiences the gift of *The Lion King*, their own *Lion King*, a *Lion King* that when they discovered it in their own rehearsal process meant as much to them as the Broadway production meant to me. And so every production became as much a learning experience as a teaching experience."

*B*ehind the beauty and splendor, *The Lion King* is a production that is fraught with danger—moving sets, complicated changes, massive machinery. When we opened in Tokyo, I was young and short on experience, and I wondered at times if we were really going to be able to safely deliver such a complex show every night. Once, facing big trouble with the machinery, I could not hide the uneasy look on my face. My colleague who was playing Scar said gently, "We cannot go onstage if the stage manager is uneasy. All you have to do is stand firmly and show confidence." I was saved! And I was able to grow from these words. I open the curtain every day with that feeling in mind.

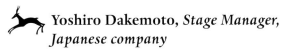

Yoshiro Dakemoto, *Stage Manager, Japanese company*

For the Record
The Lion King *Cast Albums*

There have been ten cast albums of *The Lion King* recorded around the world:

- *The Lion King* Original Broadway Cast Recording (1997)
- ライオン キング Original Tokyo Cast Recording (1999)
- *Der König Der Löwen* Original Hamburg Cast Recording (2002)
- *The Lion King* Original Dutch Cast Recording (2004)
- *Le roi lion* Original Paris Cast Recording (2007)
- *The Lion King* South African Cast Recording (2007 Live Performance CD)
- *El rey león* Original Madrid Cast (2011)
- ライオン キング New Japanese Cast Recording (2011)
- *El rey león* Original Mexico City Cast (2015)
- *The Lion King* New Dutch Cast Recording (2016)

Of all the show's international productions to date only the São Paulo, Seoul, and Shanghai (Mandarin) versions have not released cast recordings.

In 1999, when we opened *The Lion King* production in Osaka, we had the honor of having the puppeteer of the Ningyo-Joruri-Bunraku—a classical Japanese performing art that had been one of Julie Taymor's inspirations for staging this show—attend the performance. The surrounding Kansai region is the birthplace of Bunraku, and the gentleman who attended the show, Mr. Tamao Yoshida, was a designated Living National Treasure who was acclaimed as the most outstanding active puppeteer at the time. While it is said that Mr. Yoshida never watched "modern" entertainment, he highly appreciated *The Lion King* as "having a good rhythm in operating the puppets," and said that he "would like to adopt that himself within the allowable range of his art form."

 Chiyoki Yoshida, *President and Representative Director, Shiki Theatre Company*

The cast of the Shiki Theatre Company's production in Tokyo, Japan.

 Speaking Lion

The Lion King has been performed to date in nine languages: Dutch, English, French, German, Japanese, Korean, Mandarin, Portuguese, and Spanish. There were two Spanish versions created: one for Madrid and one for Mexico City. And there were two Japanese versions: one for Tokyo and one for Osaka.

The West End production of *The Lion King* won the 1999 Evening Standard Theatre Award for Theatrical Event of the Year. Additionally, it collected two Olivier Awards—one for Garth Fagan's choreography, and one for Julie Taymor's costumes.

OPPOSITE: *Young Simba (Auden Barnes) and Scar (Stephen Carlile), U.K. tour.*

LONDON, ENGLAND

OCTOBER 1999–PRESENT

The Lion King has been playing at the Lyceum Theatre in London's West End since October 1999, when the U.K. became the first English-speaking nation outside the United States to host the Pride. The 2,100-seat theater is one of London's oldest and most historic in a city with a seemingly infinite number of venerable historic show palaces, a city where Western theater was—for all intents and purposes—invented.

"In many of the theaters we use around the world, we have to do extensive remodeling," says Steve "Doc" Zorthian, the production supervisor of *The Lion King* worldwide. Having worked on several shows with Jeff

Nicholas Afoa, London, U.K.

Lee, including Julie Taymor's *Juan Darién*, Zorthian was brought on to *The Lion King* as an assistant stage manager for the original Broadway production and has worked on the show ever since.

These days he travels from country to country, usually with one of the associate directors, John Stefaniuk or Anthony Lyn, and other members of the traveling creative team, mounting and maintaining the show.

"We almost always have to make some alterations to our theaters to accommodate *The Lion King*," Zorthian says. "But in London we were coming into the Lyceum after the 1996 revival of *Jesus Christ Superstar*, and the theater, which was apparently quite threadbare before 1996, got a total refit. So, when we came along just two years later, we didn't have to do much. We did have to make adjustments to the doors into the orchestra stalls and create some aisles because of the opening procession. We almost always have to make the doors bigger."

Royal Families: The King of the Jungle and the Prince of the Realm

The first time the cast of *The Lion King* performed for a member of the British royal family was at a preview performance at the Lyceum in October of 1999. In attendance was His Royal Highness, The Prince of Wales, aka Prince Charles. The benefit performance was on behalf

of the Prince's Trust, a charitable organization founded by Charles to help young people in need in Britain. (Since its inception in 1976, some $1.4 billion has been raised by the trust.) *The Lion King* performed for Charles again in 2005, when the Lyceum hosted a Prince's Trust award ceremony.

In 2008, *The Lion King* became the first West End musical ever to be granted an encore at a Royal Variety Performance, another high-visibility annual benefit, held that year in the London Palladium on December 11. In attendance were Prince Charles as well as his consort, the Duchess of Cornwall (the former Camilla Parker Bowles).

The U.K. Tour

In addition to the West End production, Disney mounted a "U.K. Tour" from its London office, although it had an international element to it, as well. The tour kicked off September of 2012 in Bristol and played eight other cities in England: Manchester, Birmingham, Plymouth, Bradford, Liverpool, Southampton, and Sunderland. The tour also stopped off in Cardiff and Edinburgh, as well as Dublin. A last stop was made in Basel, Switzerland, where the show was also performed in English (March–October 2015), before the tour folded up its tents.

The level of detail in the costumes, makeup and puppetry is utterly staggering and Taymor creates a visual feast for the eyes aided by Garth Fagan's authentic and energetic choreography that makes you forget you are watching humans. This is blended with the subtlety of the direction that at its most powerful shows a water hole drying up with just the simplest trick and binds together a fully immersive technical feat. There is simply nothing like this musical on a production level, and the fact it stands the test of time and is yet to be bettered is proof alone of its success.

 Dom O'Hanlon, London Theatre, *from a fifteenth-anniversary review*

Stephen Carlile as Scar and Cleveland Cathnott as Mufasa face off in the U.K. tour.

I joined *The Lion King* in London in 2004. I remember when I first auditioned for the show in South Africa, I was clueless—I had no understanding what exactly I was auditioning for, and I was surprised when I got a call from the producers offering me a job in Europe! I don't think I even slept on the plane, I was so terrified, because I've never been anywhere else before—never even owned a passport.

When I joined the show, I didn't have much education; my English was not good. I left my country so young to find a better life after losing my father to a tragic accident. I had to learn to accept myself, and gain confidence and the strength to face different challenges. I used to doubt myself, I didn't believe I was good enough. Disney paved the way for me and my family, and *The Lion King* was truly a breakthrough to everything. I am proud of being a South African in the show, and I can now proclaim that through my days with *The Lion King*, I have managed to fix my own "brokenness."

Thulisile Thusi, *Ensemble, London, Hamburg, and Broadway companies*

Rafiki (Gugwana Dlamini) welcomes the animals onstage, U.K. tour.

In 2001 Young Simba was played in Toronto by Indo-Guyanese child actor Raymond Ablack, who went on to become one of the stars of the long-running Canadian television drama *Degrassi: The Next Generation* and other television programs.

TORONTO, CANADA

APRIL 2000–JANUARY 2004

Simba's next destination outside the United States was north of the border in Toronto, where *The Lion King* was licensed to Mirvish Productions, the largest theatrical promoter in Canada. There *The Lion King* played 1,560 performances at the Princess of Wales Theatre, a decidedly modern venue in the world of ornate, historic lyric theaters, featuring extensive murals by Frank Stella. It was built in 1993 by the company's founder, Ed Mirvish, who was known as "Honest Ed" after the name of his flagship discount store, Honest Ed's. (The company is now run by his son David Mirvish; the founder passed away in 2007.)

"One of the most interesting things to me about Toronto," says Doc Zorthian, "was that it was the first place we used the Pride Rock that comes in from the wings rather than up from the basement, because the Princess of Wales Theatre does not have a deep enough basement. And this became the prototype for the tours and smaller houses. Since we were in Canada, land of ice hockey, we dubbed the new set piece 'the Zamboni.'

"The worry, of course, was that it wouldn't be as magical or powerful as the original," Zorthian confesses. "But it actually works extremely well. It's an incredible piece of equipment. It's like a kid's toy snake that comes in segments or a toy train. It follows a track in the stage floor and eventually comes together as a kind of grand staircase. Offstage, it closes up like an accordion so we can store it without taking all the wing space, because when it's fully extended, it's quite massive. Of course we had to restage and rechoreograph the entire 'Circle of Life' opening and closing."

The Princess of Wales Theatre in Toronto was host to Canada's production of The Lion King.

RIGHT AND MIDDLE: *Scenes from the Stage Theater im Hafen in Hamburg.*

BOTTOM: *View of the theater from across the Elbe river.*

HAMBURG,
GERMANY

DECEMBER 2001–PRESENT

Under the leadership of Johannes "Joop" van den Ende, a retired television mogul who created *Big Brother*, *Dancing with the Stars*, and *Fear Factor*, Stage Entertainment has become Europe's largest theatrical production company. They are also one of Disney's most consistent and repeatedly successful partners, having offered *Beauty and the Beast*, *Aida*, *Tarzan*, *The Hunchback of Notre Dame*, *The Little Mermaid*, *Mary Poppins*, and *Aladdin*, as well as *The Lion King*. They're no strangers to Times Square, either; Stage Entertainment and van den Ende have been frequent Tony-winning Broadway producers (*Titanic*, *Sister Act*, *42nd Street*, *Rocky*, etc.).

In Europe, Stage operates twenty theaters in Germany, the Netherlands, France, Spain, Italy, and Russia. Stage has produced *The Lion King* not only in Hamburg but also in Paris, Madrid, and Scheveningen, a district in The Hague. Stage's first production of *The Lion King* has been running since December 2001 at the 1,800-seat Stage Theater

O ur cast is also much more specialized than other productions, most of which predominantly hire traditional musical performers from European countries. We are a melting pot of different nationalities, cultures, religions, and mentalities. We come from all social classes as well as from the fringe groups of society. We maintain close relationships with one another and are up to speed on the problems, stories, and disputes involving our colleagues. This makes it difficult to keep work-related matters exclusively at the theater and to leave everything behind after handing in the key at the stage door. On the other hand, it is an incredibly wonderful and diverse experience that teaches us tolerance, acceptance, and respect for others.

 Sonja Plesse, *Deputy Theater Director, Hamburg company*

Simba (Linda Rheretyane) and his vision of Mufasa.

Working on the same musical for fifteen years will certainly leave its mark. It was an extremely awe-inspiring experience at first, but still to this day it remains unique and unrivaled for me. After all the years, and despite numerous personal setbacks, I've never grown tired of loving *The Lion King*, the employees, and all the crazy situations that I encounter every day. Every show, in all its detail, is a new, grandiose premiere every single day. It is for me at least, with the profound effect of Lebo M.'s music, the multitude of ideas and myriad details contained in this musical, and the love of "old-fashioned" live performance. To me *The Lion King* is the crown jewel of musicals to be aspired to by every musical performer.

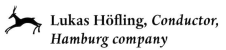 **Lukas Höfling,** *Conductor, Hamburg company*

im Hafen on the Elbe river in Hamburg, Germany's second-largest city, which is known as the Broadway of Europe.

An Emotionally Shaky Beginning

"The first day of rehearsal for *The Lion King* in Hamburg came less than two weeks after 9/11," remembers Michele Steckler, an assistant director on the original Broadway production, and subsequently a senior producer at Disney Theatrical. "The core team of associates was scattered around the globe on September eleventh, and finding our way back home to New York had called for patience and persistence. It was tough to ask everyone to get on a plane again and fly to Germany so soon after

LEFT: *Lebo M. refines the sounds of his music in Hamburg.*

OPPOSITE: *Scar and the Hyenas have been plotting together in Hamburg since 2001.*

Last year at the cast change in Hamburg, a group of refugees was invited to be our audience for the final dress rehearsal. Some of them didn't speak German yet—and quite possibly hadn't even heard of *The Lion King* musical much before that afternoon. But this group of newcomers, far from their homes, uncertain of their future, sat completely rapt and attentive for two and a half hours, absorbed in the drama unfolding onstage, bursting into a huge ovation at the end of the show. And while I sat there among these people, I felt as though I was seeing the show for the first time.

 **Mary Peterson,** *Associate Costume Designer, Broadway company*

such a horrific and traumatic event. We were all seriously shaken but determined to begin rehearsals on time, not wanting to let our partners in Germany down."

Steckler notes everyone had mixed feelings once the ball got rolling. "Walking into the rehearsal room, the excited energy and anticipation of a first rehearsal was layered with sadness and shock. A quiet focus replaced the usual beehive of activity around a first day. Yet that muted tone offered an immediate bond, a mutual respect among everyone who had made the journey to be there that day—whether from New York, South Africa, or within Germany," she adds. "People took an enormous leap to come together, and we all felt it. I sensed an appreciation for being alive and for the gift of *The Lion King* providing this opportunity to share a new beginning together. What happened that day touched everyone as we shared a world that felt more fragile than ever before. I remember there was a lot of embracing that day and a lot of love."

OPPOSITE: *Actor Rob Collins as Mufasa in the first Australian production.*

SYDNEY, AUSTRALIA

OCTOBER 2003–JUNE 2005

The production of *The Lion King* in Australia was designed as a kind of tour, but with long stops on a very limited road. The show opened at the Capitol Theatre in Sydney in October 2003 and ran over a year and a half before moving to the Regent Theatre in Melbourne for a yearlong run. Then the "Australia tour" went international, heading immediately to Shanghai to perform for three months, in English, at the Shanghai Grand Theatre. The show ran for 101 performances in Shanghai, because *Phantom of the Opera* had done a hundred, and "we wanted to beat them," says Disney's Ron Kollen with a chuckle. After a two-year hiatus, during which the Australian set was being used in South Africa, the company's production resumed outside Australia at the Taipei Arena in Taiwan, where it was seen by up to six thousand people a night for a month in August 2008.

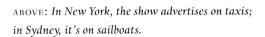

ABOVE: *In New York, the show advertises on taxis; in Sydney, it's on sailboats.*

ABOVE RIGHT: *Gugwana Dlamini as Rafiki in Australia.*

Disney revived the Australian tour for just over two years starting in 2013 (and running through 2016), playing to 1.7 million people in Sydney, Melbourne, Brisbane, and Perth. This second tour was notable for having the most multicultural cast of any Australian-produced stage musical ever, with performers from thirteen countries across five continents. The show's Simba, Nick Afoa (a New Zealander of Samoan heritage), had first auditioned for the role in 2003. But the World Cup rugby player had to wait ten years for his shot at *The Lion King*. When the tour shut its doors in Perth on February 28, 2016, Afoa moved to the West End production of *The Lion King* in London.

SCHEVENINGEN,
NETHERLANDS

APRIL 2004–AUGUST 2006 / OCTOBER 2016–PRESENT

The Circustheater in Scheveningen, a beach community that's a part of The Hague (and only forty-five minutes from Amsterdam), is the home theater of Stage

Entertainment and Dutch impresario Joop van den Ende. It's also the oldest theater in the Netherlands, having opened in 1904, and was home to a traditional circus until the 1960s. The theater has been used almost exclusively for Broadway musicals since the city sold the 1,852-seat landmark to van den Ende. His first Disney offering there was *Aida* (which ran from October 2001 to August 2003).

The Dutch have turned out to be enthusiastic musical theater goers. In a country with fifteen million inhabitants, *The Lion King* sold 1.6 million tickets in its original run, a figure that represents more than 10 percent of the population. In October 2016, Stage Entertainment opened *The Lion King* for a second time in the same location, having closed *Beauty and the Beast* to clear the stage for Simba, Pumbaa, and Timon.

> I remember the first day with the cast. We were about to do a read-through. A couple of my wonderful colleagues had already done the show, so Clement Ishmael, the musical supervisor, asked them to sing along with what they knew, just to give a sense of what the show would be like. Gugwana Dlamini, our Rafiki, was sitting next to me. She stood up and started the first notes of the show. Others joined her for the opening number. The feeling I got at that moment is indescribable. [It was] a stripped-down version of "Circle of Life" with just eight voices and a piano. I couldn't do anything else but cry.

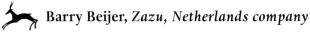 **Barry Beijer,** *Zazu, Netherlands company*

OPPOSITE: *Gaia Aikman as Nala and Naidjim Severina as Simba in the second Dutch production.*

Our production of *The Lion King* is not a "copy and paste" show. Even though the frame is the same, the heart is different. At first I was a little scared that we would get specific directions on how everything is supposed to be done, but Disney let us experiment and create our own version of the characters we play. During that beautiful journey, I learned a lot about myself. It's like one big mirror that's being held in front of me. I'm so thankful for the way our director, John Stefaniuk, worked with us. By linking the life of your character to your own, it doesn't feel as if you have to pretend to be someone else. When I enter the stage I'm not playing Nala, I *am* Nala. The costume I'm wearing is Nala's skin, but on the inside it's all me.

Gaia Aikman, *Nala, Netherlands company*

Scheveningen, Netherlands.

SEOUL, SOUTH KOREA

OCTOBER 2006–OCTOBER 2007

In 2003, the Lotte Group, an enormous multinational conglomerate headquartered in Tokyo and Seoul—and best known to consumers as the largest producer of confectionaries in South Korea—approached Disney Theatrical with their desire to build a theater capable of hosting Broadway musicals. The company owns and operates Lotte World, the planet's largest indoor theme park, which is linked to an outdoor "Magic Island" amusement park and other entertainment attractions that are spread across thirty-two acres.

Separately, the Shiki Theatre Company, Disney's producing partner in Japan, had voiced an interest in spreading its creative wings. Ultimately, both combined their efforts and reached an agreement that called for Shiki to produce *The Lion King* at Lotte Group's new Charlotte Theatre, Seoul's first commercial venue dedicated to musical theater. Unfortunately, the Korean hosts and Japanese producers found themselves at odds from the beginning.

"As the general producer," says Koichi Tanaka, Shiki's executive director, "I can say that both sides tried to foster mutual understanding, but we had several disputes with the local cast and crew. Perhaps this was caused by the cultural differences between Japan and Korea, but the Korean

Musical Theater Association initially criticized this production as a 'cultural invasion.'

"Ultimately we were able to achieve an amicable relationship with one another," Tanaka notes, "and by the end of the run, we were invited to participate in the association's festival! The production continued to run for a year, which was an epoch-making record, one that changed the history of Korean theater, and a number of the young actors from *The Lion King* production are now top stars of the Korean musical world."

"Korea and Japan have been at odds frequently in the past, so it's not that surprising that there were tensions," says Doc Zorthian. "But we were getting the show up. Unfortunately, *North* Korea started testing missiles for some reason, and every so often we'd come into the theater and we'd be missing some crew because they were in the reserves and had been called up to active service, so we had to train new crew members practically overnight. I actually found the experience to be incredibly interesting."

ABOVE: *The Charlotte Theatre in Seoul, South Korea.*

RIGHT: *The curtain call on opening night.*

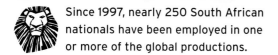
JOHANNESBURG,
SOUTH AFRICA

MAY 2007–FEBRUARY 2008

Of all the manifestations of *The Lion King* around the world, one that touched the creative team in a unique way was Disney Theatrical's first-ever production in Africa. With so much of the music and so many members of the cast around the world so identified with South Africa, it felt like the Johannesburg production was a kind of homecoming. Literally years in the making, it was a production that required the construction of a theater and the unflagging creative energies of dedicated professionals on both sides of the Atlantic. Tom Schumacher had dreamed of taking

The Lion King to South Africa, but there were so many practical and financial hurdles to jump that the dream seemed flatly impossible. But he didn't give up.

And neither did South African native Lebo M. "I just wasn't going to die before *The Lion King* went to South Africa," says Lebo. "When they said it wasn't possible, I said I'd figure it out."

Now, Lebo is a man who knows about underdogs, long shots, and bucking the odds. He began to call on his contacts in Johannesburg. One old friend, Jabu Mabuza,

The Lion King *was Disney's first theatrical production in Africa (with Buyi Zama as Rafiki).*

was building a gym at his impressive Montecasino complex. Lebo promised to deliver *The Lion King* if Mabuza would build a theater instead.

Then Lebo moved on to another old friend, who had become the CEO of Telkom. "I just begged him to give me the money that was the difference in cost between building a gym and building a world-class theater. He arranged it in half an hour.

"Then I met a man named Pieter Toerien, a lifelong producer and importer of shows to South Africa, including big musicals like *Cats* and *Phantom*," says Lebo M. "And it made sense that he and I would be the local producers of *The Lion King* in Johannesburg. I had the experience with the show and would oversee artistic matters; he had the infrastructure and expertise in finance and logistics." With a full-frontal assault by everyone involved, and the full support of the Walt Disney Company, the dream was, as Disney dreams often do, coming true. But it wasn't easy.

"To give you an idea of how complex this production was," says Toerien, "we had a tech team of about forty, half local and half veterans of other *Lion King* productions. By comparison, when we produced *Phantom of the Opera* in Johannesburg, we had only five."

And so *The Lion King* opened its tenth-anniversary production on Wednesday, June 6, 2007, at the Teatro, the new $7.5 million theater at the Tuscan-themed Montecasino. With its 1,870 seats, the Teatro is now the largest theater in Africa and one of the ten largest lyric

theaters in the world. *The Lion King* was performed by a cast of fifty-three actors, dancers, and singers—all of them from South Africa.

Opening night was emotional for everyone who had invested time, energy, talent, and heartfelt passion in the production. The deputy president of the Republic of South Africa, Phumzile Mlambo-Ngcuka, was in attendance representing the government. Disney CEO Bob Iger was on hand as was then studio chief Richard Cook. Oprah Winfrey, whose Leadership Academy for Girls had opened near Johannesburg in January of 2007, attended the opening with every single one of the boarding school's 149 students. But no one was more emotional than Lebo M.

"It was an out-of-body experience for me," he reports. "I looked at the red carpet arrivals and said, 'This looks like opening night of *The Lion King* in South Africa, so

South Africa was unique in so many ways. Basically, we were teaching people how to do theater. Clearly they didn't need to be taught South African music or languages, which we had to teach everywhere else in the world. But the South African cast didn't have the training or experience that you would have almost anywhere else, so it took a lot of care and a lot of energy to get them to a point where they were really doing *The Lion King*. And in the end, I think it was one of the most exciting productions we had done, because we had no idea what was going to happen on opening night.

 Marey Griffith, *Associate Choreographer, TLK Worldwide*

this can't be real.' From the moment Rafiki sang 'Nants' ingonyama' to begin the first act, I was hiding my tears. Twenty seconds later, I said, 'I have to go to the bathroom,' and I sobbed there like a two-month-old baby. I don't think I said more than two words to Oprah or to Tom [Schumacher] or any of the other friends and familiar faces. I was like a little zombie standing in a corner trying to figure out what was happening. It took years for me to get over the emotional enormity of seeing my dream realized."

"Johannesburg was our most challenging production ever," says Disney Theatrical's Ron Kollen, "but it was also our most beautiful. Challenging because working in South Africa and actually mounting the show proved difficult at every turn. Just finding rehearsal space big enough was difficult. And that's in addition to having to have a theater built to accommodate us.

"Plus, we were the first ones in the theater, and we were teching while the builders were still dry-walling," he recounts. "And no matter what you do in South Africa,

there winds up being at least a little racism, and you're going to feel it, and it doesn't feel good.

"Still opening night was a triumph," Kollen notes. "The company that we put together, all South African, white and black, were beautiful and got along beautifully. They knew they were doing this show that had its musical and spiritual roots in South Africa. And then doing it with so many black actors in a country where this would have been unthinkable in the days when Lebo was working on *The Lion King* film—and being successful, having been seen by over half a million people, many of whom had never seen a play before—was just wonderful.

"I can tell you one thing," Kollen adds. "The South African audience reacted to 'One by One' unlike any other audience in the world. Lebo wrote that song at the height of apartheid. And it was a universally known protest song, the gist of it being 'They are killing us, my brothers and

I have a vivid memory of being in the theater in South Africa when there were a lot of kids from the townships of Johannesburg who were given the opportunity to see *The Lion King* by corporate underwriting. And to be in South Africa, to be working on a piece that is an homage to African culture on a certain level, and to hear the laughter of those African kids who have never been in a theater, have never experienced live theater, to hear the elation of the audience. . . . You could feel the pride they felt in seeing African actors and dancers onstage singing African music. And I was so proud to have helped make the thing that brought them such joy. To have been a witness to that is something I'll never forget.

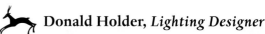 **Donald Holder,** *Lighting Designer*

sisters, one by one.' Years after the end of apartheid, Lebo changed the lyrics to the lyrics we're using in the show, turning the sadness of the original into a celebration of joy for all the people of South Africa, 'One by One.'

"Another thing we did is that every Wednesday matinee was Township Kids day. We were able to find a sponsor, so every ticket was free. These kids from the townships would never be able to do that, and it was extremely gratifying. We ran eight months, a record in South Africa. Many of the cast went on to other productions around the world. And, of course, the theater is still in use today."

Pumbaa and Timon in South Africa

"Using the model of the original casting," says Julie Taymor, "we were looking for white actors to play Pumbaa and Timon in the Johannesburg production.

After all, there are a lot of white South Africans, we thought, let's see what we get. But we couldn't find a Timon we liked, so I said, 'Well, open it up. What's the big deal?' Because there was one guy from a township outside of Cape Town who was just brilliant. So we went with a black African Timon and an Afrikaner Pumbaa, and I told them to stick to their own accents, because they are very different. So the whole production had another level of meaning that no other place has, and that was just astounding. And it made perfect sense: these two characters, when they were cast out into the jungle, essentially missed apartheid. That's what came with this casting. The audience was very aware that this does not happen, that Timon and Pumbaa can't be best friends, but the characters had no idea that they shouldn't be, in the same way that a meerkat and a warthog are an unlikely pair, but with a deeper political twist."

ABOVE: *Young Simba (Linda Dlamini) meets Pumbaa (Pierre van Heerden) and Timon (Peter Mashigo) in the South African production.*

199

PARIS, FRANCE

OCTOBER 2007–JULY 2010

The record-breaking *Le Roi Lion* in Paris, the first staging in French, was the third Stage Entertainment production in Europe. It opened at the historic Théâtre Mogador in the nineteenth arrondissement. The 1,800-seat theater was built during World War I, and U.S. President Woodrow Wilson, in town to negotiate the terms of the Treaty of Versailles, which ended the Great War, attended the theater's opening. Joop van den Ende bought the Mogador in 2005 and set about a $40 million renovation prior to staging the *Lion King* there for what turned out to be a three-year run.

"There are different things about the productions in each country," says Doc Zorthian, "and that is intentional.

This majestic Théâtre Mogador was extensively renovated to accommodate Le Roi Lion.

It's based on the culture of the country that is producing the show. Shanghai has a monkey character that was added just for that production. The Japanese productions don't have live orchestras; they do everything on a track. Some of the trims we made to the show on Broadway have not been adopted consistently by all the productions. And in every country the national character tends to come out. In Asia, the spirituality seems to be emphasized, the mysticism. In some places it's all about Timon and Pumbaa and the comedy. In Paris the show is more about the love story of Simba and Nala, and that production tended to be more romantic in tone. It may be a cliché, but when you've seen a lot of productions side by side, it's also quite evident.

"Joop van den Ende did a massive renovation at the Mogador Theatre before he put *The Lion King* in it," says Zorthian, "all new framing and rigging, totally modernizing its function, demolishing the auditorium floor and digging new basements, excavating the stage—but keeping the original look of the place. It was one of the smallest backstage areas we've ever worked with. They had to put elevators in so we could take scenery downstairs and bring other scenery up. But the show there was so charming it played like a chamber piece; it was so intimate you felt like you were right there with the actors and the puppets."

Mufasa…Meet Molière

In a ceremony held at the Folies Begère on April 28, 2008, *The Lion King* en français won three Molière Awards, the equivalent of Broadway's Tonys. In addition to recognition for costumes and lighting, Julie Taymor's brainchild was named Best Musical of the Year.

SINGAPORE

MARCH 2011–OCTOBER 2011

The Lion King production in the city-state of Singapore—nicknamed the Lion City (from the original Sanskrit for "Singapore")—was presented by BASE Entertainment, a major purveyor of live entertainment with offices in New York, Las Vegas, and Houston. Partnering with BASE, and providing the venue for this Southeast Asian debut of the show, was the Marina Bay Sands, a massive $8 billion casino/hotel/resort complex designed by Israeli-born, Canadian-educated architect Moshe Safdie.

The Lion King helps to spread values such as a friendship, respect, and collaboration, and the fact of knowing that millions of people have seen *The Lion King* around the world, and share these values, makes me more optimistic about the future of humanity.

Yolanda Pérez, *Marketing and Commercial Director, Spanish company*

OPPOSITE: *Daniela Pobega as Nala in the Madrid production.*

RIGHT: El Rey León *on the Gran Via of Spain's capital city.*

MADRID, SPAIN

OCTOBER 2011–PRESENT

Spain was the first Spanish-speaking country to produce *The Lion King*, at the Teatro Lope de Vega on Madrid's Gran Vía, known as the "Broadway of Madrid" because of its many showplaces. Produced under the aegis of Stage Entertainment, *El Rey León* has been the most successful musical in any Spanish market to date. The theater itself, built in 1947, spent much of its life as a movie house but was restored to use as a live theater in 1997. It received an additional facelift before *The Lion King* opened. In 2016, Stage Entertainment, which had been using the building since 1999, bought it outright. "When we started in Madrid," remembers Ron Kollen, "Spain was still in the midst of a deep depression from the financial effects of 2008 and 2009. I thought we would run a year and not even recoup, but it's been going strong for six."

On June 19, 2014, the coronation parade of Felipe VI drove past el Teatro Lope de Vega, and Spain's new king saluted *The Lion King* logo on the theater's marquee, one monarch acknowledging another.

The most difficult part for me was to adapt *The Lion King* to the size of the Lope de Vega Theatre stage. It was hard to find the needed space for all the elements that take action during the show. We had to "cannibalize" many spaces to make room for the costumes, the puppets, workshop, storage, and all the other uses, creating room where it didn't exist before. The first run-through of the show was a magical experience. That day, after two months of refurbishing the theater, both front of house and backstage, and two more months of rehearsals, the run-through was perfect. We didn't have to stop. Everything came together in perfect coordination.

Juan Rey, *Technical Manager, Spanish company*

What has surprised me the most has been *The Lion King*'s power to heal—oneself, and others. The rehearsal period itself was therapeutic. On a personal level, I opened up about things I hadn't talked about for more than twenty years; I was able to close wounds from my childhood. Every night I feel like the lyrics of "They Live in You" are speaking directly to me. One fan thanked me for giving her strength. She was going through cancer treatment, and she saw in Mufasa the spirituality, peace, and bravery she needed. A year later she stopped by the stage door to tell me she was cancer-free. The show still excites me as if it's the first day. It certainly has been a learning experience, but the most important thing for me has been finding a piece of me I didn't even know was missing.

 David Comrie, *Mufasa, Spanish company*

To work for *The Lion King* is a constant challenge. Nothing but the best to keep the image of the show high—it is very demanding. After so many years and so many performances, to keep the image of the show always fresh is not an easy task, but it must be done. Fortunately, working with a show that carries so much goodwill always makes opportunities to do new things possible. If there is any musical that allows exploration and trying new ways to engage people, it is *The Lion King*.

Carolina Martin, *Production Manager, Spanish company*

Being responsible for the executive production of such a big show is very challenging. The hardest thing for me was to get used to the size and complexity of *The Lion King*. The number of people involved, both in Spain and internationally, was difficult to organize. Any mistake could create delays affecting many departments. But at the end, everything worked out well and we had a wonderful opening night!

Fernando Olives, *Executive Producer, Spanish company*

Carlos Rivera has played Simba in both Madrid and Mexico City.

SÃO PAULO, BRAZIL

MARCH 2013–DECEMBER 2014

The record-breaking run of *O Rei Leão* in South America's largest city took place at the art nouveau Teatro Renault. Formerly called the Paramount Cineteatro, it opened in 1929 as the first sound cinema in Latin America. The musical was presented by the Brazil-based T4F (Time for Fun). Under the leadership of Fernando Luiz Alterio, T4F is the largest producer of live entertainment in Latin America and third largest in the world.

For the premiere Latin American production of *The Lion King*, T4F engaged the Grammy-winning Gilberto Gil, one of the most celebrated and admired musicians in the country, to write the Portuguese lyrics for the show's songs, including "Ciclo de Vida" ("Circle of Life") and "Estão em Ti" ("They Live in You"). Gil, who served as Brazil's minister of culture from 2003 to 2008, was the perfect simpatico choice for the job: his own fusion "world music" includes rock, samba, and reggae, along with multiple African styles.

"São Paulo was a challenging production," says Disney's Ron Kollen, "because Brazil is not a commercial theater capital for big shows. But we have a partner down there, Fernando Alterio, who had done *Beauty and the Beast* twice and a lot of other big shows, and he wanted to do *The Lion King*. We actually tried to dissuade him, telling him that the show was too big for his market, that he would lose money, but we finally relinquished, using an existing Australian set to help make the economics work.

"We always try to have some element of each production built in the host country," says Kollen, "so in Brazil we employed some of the many skillful seamstresses who build those elaborate Canival costumes to refresh and re-hab our whole *Lion King* wardrobe, and they did a spectacular job. We were so proud to have the show down there, and the cast was beautiful, but Fernando couldn't get the ticket price high enough to make much profit, because Brazil has a big poverty problem. In fact, our Simba in Brazil, Tiago Barbosa, was living in a favela in Rio when he walked into an open audition. He later said he made more money working on *The Lion King* than his family had ever made in their lives."

"You know," says Zorthian, "theater is really an American and British industry. We have the talent and skilled workers we need to produce anything you can think of in these two countries. But in other places, you don't have the trained people you need, and it's different in each place. In São Paulo we could not find anyone who was proficient in computerized stage automation. We ended up hiring a guy from Australia who had done the show before, and he stayed for six months to train the Brazilian crew to do automation. But dancers . . . Brazil has all the dancers you could ever need, beautiful, energetic, passionate dancers. There are a lot of Brazilians in the show all over the world, four or five of them in London, I think, and maybe the same in Hamburg. A lot of our acrobatic dancers come from Brazil."

The Brazil ensemble performing "One by One."

MEXICO CITY, MEXICO

MAY 2015–PRESENT

M y attitude and perspective as a performer have completely changed. I remind myself daily that as Rafiki, I'm the best or worst first impression of the entire performance. This has affected my view of life. I honor every performance and stay alert to the truth and the fact that I don't have a second chance to begin with the same audience—I must do it right the first time.

Charlotte Hlahatse, *Rafiki,* **Mexico company**

"Back in 2013, Tom Schumacher and I went down to Mexico," relates Ron Kollen, "because one of the promoters we knew down there, a larger-than-life gentleman called Carlos Slim, was building a theater, and he wanted to do *The Lion King*. Now, Carlos is one of the richest men in the world, *the* richest man for several years running, and he was developing a huge retail and entertainment complex in Mexico City with a shopping mall and a museum and a theater for Broadway musicals. The only problem was that no one seems to have researched what a Broadway-style theater is.

"For one thing, it was five floors belowground. It had wraparound seating, more like a symphony hall than anything else, with a raked audience on a hydraulic lift, and it had no fly tower, because there was a parking garage on top of it. And Tom told Carlos's nephew, who was our escort that day, 'Disney will never do a show here. Cameron Mackintosh will never do a show here. We can't. So if you are really serious, tear this thing down and built a proper lyric theater.'

"Within two weeks, Tom gets a visit from the Argentinian architects who had designed the whole project, and they said, 'What should we do?' They wound up gutting everything they had already built and turning the parking space into the fly tower. It only has eleven hundred seats, but that's fine. And there's now a nice park on top."

The Lion King is in its third year in Mexico City, where it is produced by OCESA, the live event sector of Mexico's enormous entertainment and media company, Grupo CIE.

ABOVE LEFT: *Charlotte Hlahatse as Mexico City's Rafiki.*

Something that surprised me was seeing all the puppets, masks, and mechanisms all together. The textures of the materials, all the different pieces that each puppet needs, this was all new to me. There were just so many puppets, mechanisms, masks, and pieces that it was hard to imagine that I would know how to use and manage them all. Knowing that I could count on professional people, and that I could learn from them how to use all the material, all the colors, all the tools was amazing to me. This is a musical that requires so many things, so many colors, so many emotions, and so much work. Every day I learn something new. You realize that you enjoy and love doing what you do—and that changes your life.

Miguel Alonso, *Puppets, Mexico company*

To my surprise, *The Lion King* turned out to be more current than I thought. The story of a tyrant ruler that allies with the enemy to reach the throne and power, the story of a woman who is forced to leave her town and home to look for help far away from her people, and the story of a man who must face his present in order to change his future. This seemed like an exact copy of the situation that México was going through with its migratory problems, the relationship between the government and the drug industry, and the part that each of us plays as citizens in addressing this problem. Telling the story of *The Lion King* turned into something fundamental for me. I was doing what I love about doing theater: I was having a dialogue about our situation, with my people, using more than just words.

 Alfonso Borbolla, *Timon, Mexico company*

There's a life before and one after *The Lion King* for everyone who has been involved in this show. There's a legend among the actors that says that whoever is blessed with being part of the show has a beautiful path ahead, full of good things waiting for them. That's because the magic of the story, the essence of the show, remains in the hearts of all of us who are part of the beautiful world of *The Lion King*.

Agustin Arguello, *Simba, Mexico company*

Flavio Medina as Scar, Carlos Rivera as Simba, and Fela Dominguez as Nala in the Mexico City production.

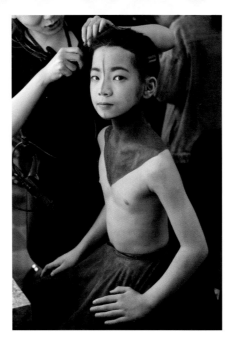

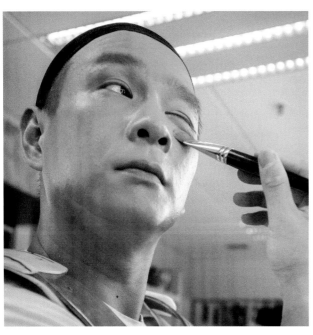

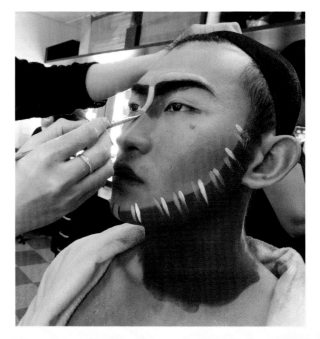

SHANGHAI, CHINA

JUNE 16, 2016–OCTOBER 2017

"We never thought we'd be able to do a production with a Chinese cast," says Ron Kollen, "because there's no such thing in China as a Broadway-style triple threat—an actor/singer/dancer. They don't know what Western musical theater is. There are no academies. There are a couple of schools in Shanghai that teach musical theater. But, surprisingly, we were able to find them. We didn't expect the show to be as good as it was. It was clearly 'up to standard' despite the low expectations we had. It was a beautiful production, and the acting was wonderful."

A New Character for a New Production in a New Disney Park

The latest Disney theme park, Shanghai Disney Resort, opened in mainland China's second most populous city on June 16, 2016. And what did a new park that is twice the size of Disneyland in Anaheim need? A brand-new production of *The Lion King*, the first-ever rendering of the musical in Mandarin, China's ancient and esteemed official language. Quite correctly, it was thought a resident company needed to speak in the host country's tongue.

But the language was not the only new thing about *The Lion King* in Shanghai, which performed at the 1,200-seat Walt Disney Grand Theatre in Disneytown, the resort's dining and retail center. For the greatly anticipated event, Julie Taymor had the idea to create the show's

first new character since its debut on Broadway in 1997, choosing the perfect beast for 2016, a year of the monkey in the Chinese zodiac: the Monkey Master, based on the mythological character called Sun Wukong (the "Monkey

OPPOSITE: *Members of the Shanghai cast meet their makeup for the first production of* The Lion King *in Mandarin.*

215

RIGHT: *Wen Xiaowei as Timon (in a Chinese headdress) and Peng Pei as Pumbaa.*

BELOW: *Wu Zi-Rong as the Monkey Master, the show's first new character since its Broadway opening.*

King") is one of the most enduring figures of Chinese legend, and he appears frequently in classic literature as well as the Beijing opera. The addition of the new character did not require alterations to the script, however, as the Monkey Master did not speak. He appeared as a champion for Simba in the young king's struggle against Scar and the dreaded hyenas. The Monkey Master's red-and-yellow costume featured modernized traditional elements and a take on the character's signature red-and-white makeup.

During the show, the Zazu actor might come to me and tell me that his bird can't open its eyes, or its wings are not functioning. The giraffe actor might say, with a little shock, that he almost fell onstage. Sometimes the Scar actor would say that his Scar mask hit him too hard. When this happened, we were like doctors, diagnosing them, treating them, and repairing them, to make sure that our actors could be 100 percent perfect onstage. Then I stood in the wings, watching and enjoying their wonderful glowing moment onstage. They made the puppets alive. And even thinking of this motivated me, every time.

 Blue Xu, *Puppet Crew, Shanghai company*

We had eight shows a week, and most of the time I was an ensemble dancer. Ensembles won't always leave an impression on the audience the way the principals do. However, I always told myself, "Don't look down on this position. It is always busy and tiring when you are being an ensemble dancer and yet ensembles are as important as principals." Knowing the fact that without ensembles the show can't go on is one of the motivations that keeps me going.

Randy Chien, *Ensemble and Standby Ed, Shanghai company*

I am so thankful that I could play Nala, and I regard the lioness as a very straightforward, strong, and gritty animal. I feel Nala has given me the strength to be stronger. She has given me the experience that I never had before. Sometimes I might feel bad when I can't be the best of me, when I am really physically tired. But when I look at the Nala puppet, I can feel the power that she is giving me, which keeps me going, and I can push myself to the limit.

Weiling Li, *Nala, Shanghai company*

Li Weiling as Nala and the ensemble Lionesses in the Shanghai production at Disney's newest park.

The final moments of the Shanghai production of **The Lion King.**

Having been educated in the West, it would be dishonest to say that I did not arrive in China with certain biases and preconceived notions toward China and its people. But slowly, through performances, rehearsals, and voice lessons, along with many laughter-filled conversations with the Chinese nationals, I had the pleasure of getting to know some of the most sensitive, thoughtful, and amazing human beings. I have always taken pride in my cultural and historical background, but now I can confidently say I have grown to love this country and its people. I have reconnected with my birthplace on both a human and spiritual level, and I cannot thank *The Lion King* enough for the opportunity.

 Lily Ling, *Associate Musical Director, Shanghai company*

More Thoughts and Feelings About *The Lion King* from Around the World

From some of the people who made it and make it run:

I was appalled when I first heard of molding masks out of carbon! I was aware of the existence of carbon as a material and knew how to mold things. However, I had always thought of this as a material for industrial products, not for creating theater! But the original creative team provided us with enthusiastic guidance. Visiting Michael Curry's studio is a fond memory of mine. Using the lightweight carbon led to more flexible thinking, free from limitations, to realize Julie Taymor's original vision.

—**Masayoshi Oosaka**, *Props, Shiki Theatre Company*

When we had decided to mount *The Lion King* in Japan, we listened to the Broadway cast album—and the door opened to a world of music we had never heard before: the distinct sounds of the African music, the Zulu language, the groovy rhythms and the tones of an array of unique percussion instruments we couldn't even name. Lebo M. visited us to give vocal lessons. His singing voice was the heartbeat of Earth itself, with its dynamism, profoundness, and direct connection to the heart.

—**Shiki Yuri Goto**, *Music Department,*
Japanese company

In 2000, I was in London for a semester of college. Our dorms were right next to Waterloo station, and we would walk past the Lyceum Theatre every day; so four of us decided we were going to wait in line for rush tickets on our day off. We ended up getting the last four "seats,"

which were standing room locations at the back of the Grand Circle. I was as far from the stage as you can get in that theater.

[But] I'll never forget watching the opening of *The Lion King* for the first time that night. I was blown away. Even in the very back corner I was totally immersed in the show. I had not experienced anything like it before in my life. Now I work for Disney Theatrical Productions in New York and have had the privilege of traveling to London several times for work. Every time I go back to the Lyceum, I visit the spot I stood that first time, and it still excites me. I feel such a connection now to the people who will be seeing *The Lion King* for the first time that night.

—**Noel Moore**, *Senior Business Analyst,*
Disney Theatrical Productions

We have a cast change process every season. It's always a stirring time for me. On one hand, you have to make hard decisions and let people go for the good of the show, and on the other hand, you welcome new people with new energy and joy. The mixing of those emotions affects me during these changes, but I have learned to overcome it and give it a positive approach.

—**Fernando Olives**, *Executive Producer,*
Spanish company

What surprised me the most about working on *The Lion King* was the level of perfection on everything. Every single detail is taken care of, everything has a sense and a reason; the designs are brilliant, from the lights to the costumes and puppets. The constant quality monitoring that the international Disney team is performing is amazing, too. It makes every performance look like opening night; it's astonishing.

—**Laura García Canelo**, *Makeup Department, Spanish company*

Backstage, every crew member wore black. The actors, of course, have colorful and varied costumes. One night, during "He Lives in You," I was in the left wing. Suddenly, the lights and music burst on, lighting the whole stage. Offstage, the stage manager and crews from props started to dance in the wings with the actors dancing onstage. The dark shadows and the colorful stage made up a wonderful picture. At that moment, I felt like it was the most beautiful dance in the world. Formerly, as an actor, I hardly paid attention to the people in black. At *The Lion King*, I gradually found that if actors are stars, the people in black are the dark night sky. Darkness allows stars to shine brighter. When Shannon hands the pole puppet to me, when ManMan helps me to put on Ed's costume, when Birdy helps me with Timon's tail, when Knife shouts, "Ready, go!" beside me, it represents the connection between two types of work—moreover, the connection between two types of worlds.

—**Lester Zhang**, *Ed, Shanghai company*

There are musicals that can make you happy, and those that make you cry. There is also this kind of musical which can show you the way, just like *The Lion King*. Just like the lyrics "When you were by my side, guiding my way." I no longer talk with my father very often. I am glad that *The Lion King* appeared, guiding my way. Thank you, *Lion King*, the father I found at the age of thirty!

—**Xiaolin Yu**, *Ensemble, Shanghai company*

In Mexico City, the theater we play in is built underground. The stage is located on the minus-fifth floor. Imagine loading in a show in the fifth story of a building—now picture that turned upside down! All the set pieces have to literally fly down with a crane from the ground level to the minus-five floor. It was so much fun getting the elephant into the theater; we had our own Dumbo landing in our stage, bringing all the Disney magic with him.

—**Jaime Matarredona**, *Production Supervisor, Mexico company*

The Lion King tells us about the most pressing matters of our time. I was most impressed by the image of a land wasted, devastated because of the greed and stupidity of a bad ruler. It is about the death of hope—and then again about its rebirth. It is a reminder for us of being part of a bigger plan, that we have to take care of the seemingly lesser beings in nature, because we are inextricably linked. The multicultural music itself conveys this profound spirituality. Never before have I ended performances so uplifted.

—**Isaac Saúl**, *Resident Musical Director, Mexico company*

The Lion King *Family*

In two decades, *The Lion King* in its many incarnations has been home to hundreds if not thousands of talented performers, artists, and theatre craftspeople. They all belong to a single international "family," and unlike most Broadway productions, the cast, crew, and creative contributors on *The Lion King* frequently spend many years with the show.

Ensemble member Lindiwe Dlamini is the sole remaining member of *The Lion King*'s original Broadway cast, and consequently holds the world record for most performances by an actress in *The Lion King*. She is now married to fellow South African Bongi Duma, who is also in the New York ensemble but who was originally cast for the German production in Hamburg. They are one of many couples who met while working on *The Lion King* who now have young Simbas and Nalas of their own.

Actors playing Mufasa seem particularly fond of long runs. Alton Fitzgerald White holds the record, with 4,308 performances over thirteen years in the role on the Gazelle Tour, in Las Vegas, and on Broadway. Other long-lived Mufasas include

Alton Fitzgerald White as Mufasa.

Nathaniel Stampley from the Broadway, West End (London), and North American touring companies; David Comrie (Madrid); and Jean-Luc Guizonne, who performed as Simba's sagacious dad in Paris, Singapore, and Hamburg.

Kissy Vaughan holds the current title for most performances as Nala, having played the role for nine consecutive years, starting with the Gazelle Tour of North America, then on Broadway for six years, ending her run in Las Vegas.

Family members who have performed in the most productions around the world include Buyi Zama, who has performed Rafiki on Broadway and on tour in North America as well as in London, South Africa, Australia, and China; and Nosipho Nkonqa, who first performed in the original Dutch production and then went on as an ensemble member in South Africa, Taiwan, Singapore, and in the U.K., both in London and on tour.

Kissy Vaughan as Nala.

Unique in the world, Japan's two concurrent productions (Tokyo and tour) are cast from a fixed company of actors who play in repertory with other Shiki-produced shows, some of them also by Disney. The original Rafiki, for example, has been performing in *The Lion King* since 1999, but not continuously; she's also played many other roles, including Ursula in *The Little Mermaid*. And last year, Shiki's two Aladdins both also played Simba.

Carlos Rivera, who has performed Simba over a thousand times, in Madrid and Mexico City, is the only *Lion King* actor whose voice can be heard on two different recordings, the cast albums of both the Spanish and Mexican productions (which are two different versions of the text).

Two actresses have performed *The Lion King* in three different languages: Ntsepa Pitjeng, who played Rafiki in Mandarin in Shanghai, was also in the São Paulo and London productions; Portia Manyike was a member of the ensemble in France, Brazil, and Mexico.

The Lion King family also boasts a set of twins. Nokubonga Khuzwayo appeared in Johannesburg, Hamburg, London, Broadway, Las Vegas, and the

Gaia Aikman as Adult Nala.

Gazelle Tour. Her sister, Nokwanda Khuzwayo has appeared in São Paulo and Shanghai.

Gaia Aikman is the first actress to perform Nala in *The Lion King* as both a child and an adult. She was one of the kids from the first Dutch production in 2004–2006 and was cast as the grown incarnation of the fearless lioness in the current Netherlands revival. Jade Ewen, who played Young Nala in the West End has not yet played Adult Nala, but she has been starring as Jasmine in London's *Aladdin*. (So far none of the Young Simbas has grown into the adult role, but several have graduated to the ensemble.)

Members of the family sometimes leave *The Lion King* for other Disney shows: Heather Headley, the original Nala from the Broadway company, left the show to perform the title role of *Aida*, a part that won her a Tony Award for Best Performance by an Actress in a Musical. Prior to snarling as Scar on the Gazelle tour and on Broadway, Patrick Page played Lumiere in *Beauty and the Beast*, both on Broadway and on the road, and went on to play Frollo in *The Hunchback of Notre Dame*. Tom Alan Robbins, the all-time longest-running Pumbaa (over 5,500 performances over thirteen years), later did *Newsies* on Broadway.

Carlos Rivera as Simba.

ACKNOWLEDGMENTS

Like animated movies and Broadway shows, books are collaborations. The "author" gets his name on the cover, but there are many behind-the-scenes contributors without whom the book would have remained a random assortment of handwritten scribbles and computer files.

The "author" of *The Lion King: Twenty Years on Broadway and Around the World* is grateful to frequent partner in crime Wendy Lefkon, editorial director of Disney Editions, a great talent and a great friend, as well as her eagle-eyed team of copy editors, proofreaders, and fact-checkers, annoying as they sometimes are. And to Clark and Gregory Wakabayashi, the unrivaled siblings of Welcome Enterprises, and the talented duo responsible for the design and production of this and so many other glorious Disney titles. The book would not have been possible without the cheerful diligence of Jeff Kurtti, who did much research, wrote many sections of the book, and wrangled the quotations from *The Lion King* company members from around the world. Steven Downing, VP, Licensed Brands & Merchandising at Disney Theatrical, brought his unique photographic vision across all *The Lion King* productions. Max Garvin, assistant manager, Merchandise Projects, worked tirelessly and fielded questions, produced answers, assembled raw material, and rode herd on the massive Disney archive of *The Lion King* visual material— which you might imagine to be exhaustive, although the "author" and the Brothers Wakabayashi still managed to

request images that had to be snatched from the ether.

Many thanks go to members of *The Lion King* creative team for being willing to be interviewed yet again and to past and present members of Disney Theatrical Productions for assistance and support (in the following alphabetical and probably incomplete list): Ken Cerniglia, Hunter Chancellor, Michael Cohen, Dennis Crowley, Jack Eldon, Gregory Hanoian, Julia Haverkate, Ron Kollen, Jeff Lee, Aubrey Lynch II, Anne Quart, Christopher Recker, Thomas Schlenk, Seth Stuhl, Peter Schneider, Julie Taymor, Lisa M. Weiner, and Doc Zorthian. And to my friend and dance critic Eva Yaa Asentewaa.

Finally, the "author" wishes to thank Thomas Schumacher, president and producer of Disney Theatrical Productions, for keeping things light (even though they sometimes get serious); for taking his job and his art seriously, indeed; for his endless contributions to the Broadway and greater human community; for his stewardship of the principle that nice people make good art; for the capacity to feel deep emotion about the armies of individuals who contribute to his work product; for his fidelity to his friends and loved ones; for having never wavered from his essence as his public profile and his fortunes increased; for holding on to the capacity to be enchanted, delighted, and surprised; and for giving the "author" an opportunity to actually be one for more than twenty years of writing about Disney on Broadway. *You call that a roar?* I do.

—Michael Lassell, *New York City, 2017*

Gugwana Dlamini as Rafiki, London company.